MW00453815

CLASSIC SERMONS
ON
THE LORD'S PRAYER

The Kregel Classic Sermons Series

CLASSIC SERMONS ON THE LORD'S PRAYER

Compiled by
Warren W. Wiersbe

kregel
PUBLICATIONS

Grand Rapids, MI 49501

Classic Sermons on the Lord's Prayer
Compiled by Warren W. Wiersbe

© 2000 by Kregel Publications. All rights reserved. No part of this book may be reproduced, stored in a retrieval system, or transmitted in any form or by any means—electronic, mechanical, photocopy, recording, or otherwise—without written permission of the publisher, except for brief quotations in printed reviews.

Published by Kregel Publications, a division of Kregel, Inc., P.O. Box 2607, Grand Rapids, MI 49501. Kregel Publications provides trusted, biblical publications for Christian growth and service. Your comments and suggestions are valued.

For more information about Kregel Publications, visit our web site at: www.kregel.com

Cover photo: © PhotoDisc

ISBN 0-8254-4086-6

Printed in the United States of America
1 2 3 4 5 / 04 03 02 01 00

Contents

List of Scripture Texts

Preface

THE *Kregel Classic Sermons Series* is an attempt to assemble and publish meaningful sermons from master preachers about significant themes.

These are *sermons,* not essays or chapters taken from books about themes. Not all of these sermons could be called great, but all of them are *meaningful.* They apply the truths of the Bible to the needs of the human heart, which is something that all effective preaching must do.

While some are better known than others, all of the preachers whose sermons I have selected had important ministries and were highly respected in their day. The fact that a sermon is included in this volume does not mean that either the compiler or the publisher agrees with or endorses everything that the man did, preached, or wrote. The sermon is here because it has a valuable contribution to make.

These are sermons about *significant* themes. The pulpit is no place to play with trivia. The preacher has thirty minutes in which to help mend broken hearts, change defeated lives, and save lost souls; he can never accomplish this demanding ministry by distributing homiletical tidbits. In these difficult days we do not need clever pulpiteers who discuss the times; we need dedicated ambassadors who will preach the eternities.

The reading of these sermons can enrich your spiritual life. The studying of them can enrich your skills as an interpreter and expounder of God's truth. However God uses these sermons in your life and ministry, my prayer is that His church around the world will be encouraged and strengthened by them.

WARREN W. WIERSBE

The Praying Christ

Alexander Maclaren (1826–1910) was one of Great Britain's most famous preachers. While pastoring the Union Chapel, Manchester (1858–1903), he became known as "the prince of expository preachers." Rarely active in denominational or civic affairs, Maclaren invested his time in studying the Word in the original languages and in sharing its truths with others in sermons that are still models of effective expository preaching. He published a number of books of sermons, and the climax of his ministry was publication of the monumental *Expositions of Holy Scripture*.

This message was taken from his *Expositions of the Gospel of Luke*, reprinted by Baker Book House in 1974.

1

The Praying Christ

As he was praying in a certain place, when he ceased, one of his disciples said unto him, Lord, teach us to pray. (Luke 11:1)

It is noteworthy that we owe our knowledge of the prayers of Jesus principally to the evangelist Luke. There is, indeed, one solemn hour of supplication under the quivering shadows of the olive trees in Gethsemane that is recorded by Matthew and Mark as well. Though the fourth gospel passes over that agony of prayer, it gives us, in accordance with its ruling purpose, the great chapter that records His priestly intercession. But in addition to these instances, the first gospel furnishes but one instance and the second but two references to the subject. All the others are found in Luke.

I need not point out how this fact tallies with the many other characteristics of the third gospel, which mark it as eminently the story of the Son of Man. The record that traces our Lord's descent to Adam rather than to Abraham, which tells the story of His birth and gives us all we know of the "child Jesus," which records His growth in wisdom and stature and has preserved a multitude of minute points bearing on His true manhood, as well as on the tenderness of His sympathy and the universality of His work, most naturally emphasizes that most precious indication of His humanity—His habitual prayerfulness. The gospel of the King, which is the first gospel; or of the Servant, which is the second; or of the Son of God, which is the fourth, had less occasion to dwell on this. Royalty, practical obedience, and divinity are their respective themes. Manhood is Luke's, and he is ever pointing us to the kneeling Christ.

Consider, then, for a moment, how precious the prayers of Jesus are, as bringing Him very near to us in His true manhood. There are deep and mysterious truths involved with which we do not meddle now. But there are also plain and surface truths that are very helpful and blessed. We thank God for the story of His weariness when He sat on the well and of His slumber when, worn out with a hard day's work, He slept on the hard, wooden pillow in the stern of the fishing boat among the nets and the litter. It brings Him near to us when we read that He thirsted and nearer still when the immortal words fall on our wondering ears, "Jesus wept." But even more precious than these indications of His true participation in physical needs and human emotion is the great evidence of His prayers, that He too lived a life of dependence, communion, and submission. It is also precious that in our religious life, as in all our life, He is our pattern and forerunner. As the epistle to the Hebrews puts it, He shows that He is not ashamed to call us brothers and sisters by this, that He too avows that He lives by faith. By His life—and surely preeminently by His prayers—He declares, "I will put my trust in Him." We cannot think of Christ too often or too absolutely as the object of faith and as the hearer of our cries. But we may, and some of us do, think of Him too seldom as the pattern of faith and as the example for our devotion. We should feel Him a great deal nearer us and the fact of His manhood would not only be grasped more clearly by orthodox believers but also would be felt in more of its true tenderness if we gave more prominence in our thoughts to that picture of the praying Christ.

Another point that may be suggested is that the highest,

holiest life needs specific acts and times of prayer. A certain fantastical and overstrained spirituality is not rare, which professes to have gotten beyond the need of such beggarly elements. Some tinge of this colors the habits of many people who are scarcely conscious of its presence, and it makes them somewhat careless as to forms and times of public or private worship. I do not think that I am wrong in saying that there is a growing laxity in that matter among people who are really trying to live Christian lives. We may well take the lesson that Christ's prayers teach us, for we all need it, that no life is so high, so holy, so full of habitual communion with God that it can afford to do without the hour of prayer, the secret place, the uttered word. If we are to "pray without ceasing," by the constant attitude of communion and the constant conversion of work into worship, we must certainly have, and we shall undoubtedly desire, special moments when the daily sacrifice of doing good passes into the sacrifice of our lips. The devotion that is to be diffused through our lives must be first concentrated and evolved in our prayers. These are the gathering-grounds that feed the river. The life that was all one long prayer needed the mountaintop and the nightly converse with God. He who could say, "The Father hath not left me alone; for I do always those things that please him" (John 8:29), felt that He must also have the special communion of spoken prayer. What Christ needed we cannot afford to neglect.

Thus, Christ's own prayers do, in a very real sense, "teach us to pray." But it strikes me that if we will take the instances in which we find Him praying and try to classify them in a rough way, we may gain some hints worth laying to heart. Let me attempt this briefly now.

The Praying Christ Teaches Us to Pray
as a Rest After Service

The evangelist Mark gives us, in his brief, vivid way, in his first chapter a wonderful picture of Christ's first Sabbath day of ministry in Capernaum. It was crowded with work. The narrative goes hurrying on through the busy hours, marking the press of rapidly succeeding calls by its constant reiteration—"straightway," "immediately," "forthwith," "anon," "immediately." He teaches in the synagogue. Without breath or pause, He heals a man with an unclean spirit. Then, at once, He passes to Simon's house and, as soon as He enters, has to listen to the story of how the wife's mother lay sick of a fever. They might have let Him rest for a moment, but they are too eager, and He is too pitying, for delay. As soon as He hears, He helps. As soon as He bids it, the fever departs. As soon as she is healed, the woman is serving them. There can have been but a short snatch of such rest as such a house could afford. Then when the shadows of the western hills began to fall upon the blue waters of the lake and the sunset ended the restrictions of the Sabbath, He is besieged by a crowd full of sorrow and sickness, and all about the door they lie, waiting for its opening. He could not keep it shut any more than His heart or His hand, and so all through the short twilight and deep into the night He toils among the dim, prostrate forms. What a day it had been of hard toil, as well as of exhausting sympathy! And what was His refreshment? An hour or two of slumber and then, "in the morning, rising up a great while before day, he went out, and departed into a solitary place, and there prayed" (Mark 1:35).

In the same way we find Him seeking the same repose after another period of much exertion and strain on body and mind. He had withdrawn Himself and His disciples from the bustle that Mark describes so graphically. "There were many coming and going, and they had no leisure so much as to eat" (Mark 6:31). So, seeking quiet, He takes them across the lake into the solitudes on the other side. But the crowds from all the villages near its head catch sight of the boat in crossing and hurry round, and there they all are at the landing place, as eager and exacting as ever. He throws aside the purpose of rest, and all day long, wearied as He was, "taught them many things" (Mark 4:2). The closing of day brings no respite. He thinks of their hunger before His own fatigue and will not send them away fasting. So He ends that day of labor by the miracle of feeding the five thousand. The crowds gone to their homes, He can at last think of Himself. What is His rest? He loses not a moment in "constraining" His disciples to go away to the other side, as if in haste to remove the last hindrance to something that He had been longing to get to. "And when he had sent them away, he departed into a mountain to pray" (Mark 6:46; cf. Matt. 14:23).

That was Christ's refreshment after His toil. So He blended contemplation and service, the life of inward communion and the life of practical obedience. How much more do we need to interpose the soothing and invigorating influences of quiet communion between the acts of external work, since our work may harm us as His never did Him. It may disturb and dissipate our communion with God. It may weaken the very motive from which it should arise. It may withdraw our gaze from God and fix it upon ourselves. It may puff us up with the conceit of our own powers, or it may fret us with the annoyances of resistance. It may depress us with the consciousness of failure and, in a hundred other ways, may waste and wear away our personal religion. The more we work the more we need to pray. In this day of activity there is great danger, not of doing too much, but of praying too little for so much work. These two—work and prayer, action and contemplation—are twin sisters. Each pines without the other. We are ever tempted to cultivate one or the other disproportionately. Let us imitate Him who sought the mountaintop as His refreshment after toil but never left duties undone or sufferers unrelieved in pain. Let us imitate Him who turned from the joys of contemplation to the joys of service without a murmur when His disciples broke in on His solitude with, "All men seek for thee" (Mark 1:37), but never suffered the outward work to blunt His desire for, nor to encroach on the hour of, still communion with His Father. Lord, teach us to work; Lord, teach us to pray.

The Praying Christ Teaches Us to Pray as a Preparation for Important Steps

Although more than one gospel tells us of the calling of the Twelve, the gospel of the manhood alone narrates that on the eve of that great epoch in the development of Christ's kingdom, "He went out into a mountain to pray, and continued all night in prayer to God" (Luke 6:12). Then, "when it was day" (Luke 6:13), He calls to Him His disciples and chooses the Twelve.

A similar instance occurs, at a later period, before another great epoch in His course. The great confession made by Peter, "Thou art the Christ, the Son of the living God" (Matt. 16:16), was drawn forth by our Lord to serve as the basis for His bestowment on the apostles of large spiritual powers and for the teaching, with much increased detail and clearness, of His approaching sufferings. In both aspects it distinctly marks a new stage. Concerning it, too, we read, and again in Luke alone (9:18), that it was preceded by solitary prayer.

Thus, He teaches us where and how we may get the clear insight into circumstances and men that may guide us aright. Bring your plans, your purposes to God's throne. Test them by praying about them. Do nothing large or new—nothing small or old, either, for that matter—until you have asked there, in the silence of the secret place, "Lord, what wilt thou have me to do?" (Acts 9:6). There is nothing more bitter to parents than when children begin to take their own way without consulting them. Do you take counsel of your Father and have no secrets from Him? It will save you from many a blunder and many a heartache. It will make your judgment clear and your step assured, even in new and difficult ways, if you will learn from the praying Christ to pray before you plan and take counsel of God before you act.

The Praying Christ Teaches Us to Pray as the Condition of Receiving the Spirit and the Brightness of God

There were two occasions in the life of Christ when visible signs showed His full possession of the Divine Spirit and the luster of His glorious nature. There are large and perplexing questions connected with both, on which I have no need to enter. At His baptism the Spirit of God descended visibly and abode on Jesus. At His transfiguration His face shone as the light, and His garments were radiant as sunlit snow. Now on both these occasions our gospel, and our gospel alone, tells us that it was while Christ was in the act of prayer that the sign was given: "Jesus also being baptized, and praying, the heaven was opened, and the Holy Ghost descended" (Luke 3:21–22). "As he prayed, the fashion of his countenance was altered, and his raiment was white and glistering" (9:29).

Whatever difficulty may surround the first of these narratives especially, one thing is clear: in both of them was a true communication from the Father to the man Jesus. And another thing is, I think, clear, too: that our evangelist meant to lay stress on the preceding act as the human condition of such communication. So if we would have the heavens opened over our heads and the dove of God descending to fold its white wings and brood over the chaos of our hearts until order and light come there, we must do what the Son of Man did—pray. And if we would have the fashion of our countenances altered, the wrinkles of care wiped out, the traces of tears dried up, the blotches of unclean living healed, and all the brands of worldliness and evil exchanged for the name of God written on our foreheads, and the reflected glory irradiating our faces, we must do as Christ did—pray. So, and only so, will God's Spirit fill our hearts, God's brightness flash in our faces, and the vesture of heaven clothe our nakedness.

The Praying Christ Teaches Us to Pray as the Preparation for Sorrow

Here all three of the evangelists tell us the same sweet and solemn story. It is not for us to penetrate further than they carry us into the sanctities of Gethsemane. Jesus, though hungering for companionship in that awful hour, would take no man with Him there. He still says, "Sit ye here, while I go and pray yonder" (Matt. 26:36). But as we stand afar off, we catch the voice of pleading rising through the stillness of the night, and the solemn words tell us of a Son's confidence, of a man's shrinking, of a Savior's submission. The very spirit of all prayer is in these broken words. That was truly "the Lord's Prayer" that He poured out beneath the olives in the moonlight. It was heard when strength came from heaven, which He used and "prayed more earnestly" (Luke 22:44). It was heard when, the agony past and all the conflict ended in victory, He came forth with that strange calm and dignity to give Himself first to His captors and then to His executioners, the ransom for the many.

As we look upon that agony and these tearful prayers, let us not only look with thankfulness but also let that kneeling Savior teach us that in prayer alone can we be forearmed against our lesser sorrows. Let Him teach us that strength to bear flows into the heart that is opened in supplication, and that a sorrow which we are made able to endure is more truly conquered than a sorrow which we avoid. We have all a cross to carry and a wreath of thorns to wear. If we want to be fit for our Calvary— may we use that solemn name?—we must go to our Gethsemane first.

So the Christ who prayed on earth teaches us to pray. The Christ who intercedes in heaven helps us to pray and presents our poor cries, acceptable through His sacrifice and fragrant with the incense from His own golden censer.

> O Thou by whom we come to God,
> The Life, the Truth, the Way;
> The path of prayer Thyself hast trod
> Lord! teach us how to pray.

NOTES

The Pattern Prayer

George Campbell Morgan (1863–1945) was the son of a British Baptist preacher and preached his first sermon when he was thirteen years old. He had no formal training for the ministry, but his tireless devotion to the study of the Bible helped him to become one of the leading Bible teachers of his day. Rejected by the Methodists, he was ordained into the Congregational ministry. He was associated with Dwight L. Moody in the Northfield Bible conferences and was an itinerant Bible teacher. He is best known as the pastor of the Westminster Chapel, London (1904–1917 and 1933–1943). During his second term there, he had Dr. D. Martyn Lloyd-Jones as his associate.

Morgan published more than sixty books and booklets, and his sermons are found in *The Westminster Pulpit* (London: Hodder and Stoughton, 1906–1916). This sermon is the second of four messages on the Lord's Prayer that Morgan gave at British Keswick in 1906, recorded in *The Ministry of Keswick*, first series, edited by Herbert F. Stevenson, and published in 1963 by Zondervan Publishing House.

2

The Pattern Prayer

After this manner therefore pray ye. Our Father who art in heaven, Hallowed by thy name. Thy kingdom come. Thy will be done, as in heaven, so on earth. (Matthew 6:9–10 ASV)

LET US TURN AGAIN TO LUKE 11:1–4, "And it came to pass, as he was praying in a certain place, that when he ceased, one of his disciples said unto him, Lord, teach us to pray, even as John also taught his disciples. And he said unto them, When ye pray, say, Father, hallowed be thy name. Thy kingdom come. Give us day by day our daily bread. And forgive us our sins; for we ourselves also forgive every one that is indebted to us. And bring us not into temptation."

Now we turn back to the Manifesto of the King, Matthew 6:9–13: "After this manner therefore pray ye. Our Father who art in heaven, Hallowed be thy name. Thy kingdom come. Thy will be done, as in heaven, so on earth. Give us this day our daily bread. And forgive us our debts, as we also have forgiven our debtors. And bring us not into temptation, but deliver us from the evil"—I resolutely omit the word *one* there—"deliver us from the evil."

Notice the place that this prayer occupies. First, in answer to the request of one of His disciples, made on behalf of all of them, that He would teach them to pray, our Lord gives them certain sentences out of the prayer, which you have fully in the midst of the Manifesto. I know that it is extremely difficult to arrange these gospel stories chronologically—and I warn all Bible students against harmonies of the Gospels, except for reasons of reference, which are not very important—for the harmony of the Gospels is personal and not chronological. But, so far as one may attempt that, some things are perfectly patent. I think you will find that the answer of our Lord in Luke was subsequent to the delivery of His Manifesto to His disciples as chronicled in the gospel of Matthew. If that be so, then when they asked Him to teach them to pray, He took some of the sentences that were already familiar to them and repeated them—not all, but some. We go back to the prayer as it is found in the gospel of Matthew. We remember, first of all, its place. Think for a moment, therefore, of those who had to use this prayer.

Now, I am familiar with the fact that many of God's dear children seem to find some difficulty in making use of this prayer at all. I want to speak with all kindness and with all respect for their convictions when I say that, personally, I do not understand them—neither can I share them. I am not going to discuss all the reasons advanced against the use of the prayer by Christians. I have been told that we do not have to use the prayers because we do not now need to seek for daily forgiveness. I am afraid that the people who say that do not know their own hearts nor the nature of the debt and the debtor. Then, in the next place, I have been told that we are not to pray this prayer because the measure of forgiveness indicated here is neither the measure nor the basis of our forgiveness. That, again, is to forget that this prayer never ought to be breathed by man, woman, or child outside the kingdom. It is the prayer of the disciple. I would never imagine that we had any authority to tell a man who had never yielded to the King that he must ask to be forgiven upon the basis of his own forgiving. It is impossible to begin with. We shall come to that point later; therefore, I pass it by now.

But, in the third place—and with this view I have more sympathy than with any other—it is objected that this is not the prayer of the church; it is the prayer of the kingdom. It is most important that we should maintain in our teaching the distinction between these dispensations and methods of our God, between the church and the kingdom, and so forth. I am not going to discuss those distinctions now, but I want to remind you that when, for the time being, this day of grace (an interpolation upon the days and times and seasons of the ancient prophets, and of the Son of God) dawned, all the principles of the kingdom were committed to the church for keeping and for manifestation. I feel it is because we have lost sight of this that we have lost a great deal of power in all our work—missionary, evangelistic, and every other sort of work. That, again, I cannot discuss now. I would simply say that the facts of the kingdom of God—that being, as I understand it, the broadest phrase it is possible to use; larger, in some senses than "the kingdom of heaven" and certainly larger than the phrase "the church" in the broadest sense—all the principles of the kingdom of God are manifested in the world today through the church and only through the church. The church has a twofold business: (1) proclaiming the evangel for the gathering out of the church of the firstborn; and (2) so proclaiming the evangel as to prepare for another age and dispensation when God, by other methods, will move on toward the restitution of all things.

Therefore, it seems to me that this prayer is peculiarly ours, just as the whole Manifesto, for the time being, is ours. That, also, is important. I pause one moment because I am about to take the prayer out of that Manifesto to say that the Sermon on the Mount is only obeyed and realized today within the Christian church. It is the uttermost folly to preach it outside. Jesus never said to the promiscuous multitude, "Ye are the salt of the earth," and He never laid an ethic upon unregenerate man which that man was unable to understand and obey. To say that the Manifesto is realized and obeyed only within the church, the place for the great prayer being avowedly in the

church, does not express all the church's meaning. Our vocation, finally, is in the heavenlies; but our present vocation is
here and has to do with the earth. I believe most strongly that
the taunt of being "other-worldly" is one of which we are altogether too much afraid. When the church fails to be "other-
worldly," it loses the power to touch this world in all its dire
need. While that is true, we have also been in danger of for-
getting our responsibility to the present world, and out of that
has come our lack of missionary zeal, enthusiasm, and endeavor.

Now let us turn to the prayer itself. There are some very
simple things concerning its structure to which I desire first to
draw your attention. You will observe that the Revised Version
has omitted the closing doxology. This I am not going to discuss, but I believe the omission to be thoroughly justified. I
was interested to find a little while ago so conservative and
saintly an expositor as Hengstenberg say there can be no doubt
that the final doxology was not in the original text, but it is so
full of beauty that we had better leave it where it is. We all
sympathize with that feeling, and I never omit the doxology
when using the prayer. But, for the sake of studying the prayer
as Jesus gave it, we must omit the doxology.

In this prayer, then, in the first place, there is a general invocation: "Our Father which art in heaven." Then, immediately
following, there are six petitions. I should like to warn young
Bible students against hunting for "sevens" in the Bible. When
they *are* there, they are always significant; but when they are
not there, do not make them. First of all, you have three petitions ending with a qualifying phrase: "Thy name be hallowed,
Thy kingdom come, Thy will be done." I put them in that way
to indicate that the final phrase qualifies the whole of those
petitions and not merely one. That phrase is *As in heaven, so on
earth*. Then you have three other petitions, connected by the
word *and*–"Give us this day our daily bread; *and* forgive us our
debts, as we also have forgiven our debtors; *and* bring us not
into temptation, but deliver us from the evil." Now, I am not
intending to deal with the details of these petitions, especially

the details of the second three. I simply ask you to mark the fact of a first three and a last three. It is too late in the day to change our method of reciting the great prayer, yet I always feel the desire that our great congregations should recite it as it is written. If we cannot recite it in that form, at least we might form the habit of reciting it reverently and slowly. Nothing has shocked me more than the way in which we get through this prayer. I like to have a solemn pause upon every sentence so that we may think what we are doing as we pray this great prayer. When it has been prayed intelligently, there is nothing left that we can pray for. We have swept the whole realm of prayer.

Jesus has gathered into these sentences—all familiar to His hearers long before—and has put into perfect form the whole effect of prayer. First, three petitions and then another three. What is the difference between them? You have noticed, of course, that the first three petitions have to do wholly with the purpose and the program of God: "*Thy* name be hallowed. *Thy* kingdom come. *Thy* will be done, as in heaven, so on earth." You notice that the second three petitions have to do wholly with the probationary pilgrimages of His people: "Give us this day our daily bread; and forgive us our debts, as we also have forgiven our debtors; and bring us not into temptation, but deliver us from the evil."

Without pausing any further, let me ask you to remember that, if we catch this structure and its significance, we have a philosophy of prayer that is of the utmost importance. According to the revelation of Jesus' prayer, it is not, first, a method by which I may obtain supply for my own need. Prayer is, first, the method by which God brings me into cooperation with Himself for the accomplishment of His purpose in the world, so that the underlying principle of life is also the underlying principle of prayer. Just as Jesus said in this selfsame Manifesto concerning the life of the subjects of His kingship: "Seek ye first his kingdom, and his righteousness; and all these things shall be added unto you" (Matt. 6:33), so when He gives me the pattern of prayer He says, in effect, seek first the kingdom of God and these things of your need shall be added to you. Test your prayer by that. How does it come out? How many of us pray for everything that touches our own need and, if we have a few moments to spare, we pray for the missionaries. Christ says, "First God's kingdom." It is not a passion to be kept that I may save myself and get into His heaven presently—a perfectly right desire—but the first thing is a passion for the coming of His kingdom and the accomplishment of His purpose in the world. That is the first, great, broad revelation suggested to us by Jesus when we take up the great prayer.

I have already referred in a previous study to the wonderful verse in Luke: "Fear not, little flock, for it is your Father's good pleasure to give you the kingdom" (Luke 12:32). Now mark how this works out in your prayer. You address your prayer to the Father, and pray first for the coming of His kingdom; then you pray for the provision of His shepherd love, for all the pathway of your pilgrimage.

Now, let us look at the first part of this prayer, which has to do with the purpose and the program of God. Notice the bounding words found in the invocation and in the qualifying phrase with which the three petitions end—"Our Father which art in heaven"; and the first petitions close thus, "as in heaven so on earth." The word that naturally arrests our attention is *heaven*, occurring in the invocation and in the qualifying phrase of the first three petitions.

Now, we may seem to be making a digression, but I want to think of the word *heaven* for a moment in its use in the New Testament. Turn with me, therefore, to Matthew 6:26: "Behold the birds of the heaven." You notice the difference. Instead of "of the air," I used "of the heaven," which is a literal translation: "Behold the birds of the heaven, that they sow not, neither do they reap, nor gather into barns; and your heavenly Father feedeth them." Now turn to Acts 2:19: "I will show wonders in the heaven above, and signs on the earth beneath; blood, and fire, and vapor of smoke." Now, 2 Corinthia... 12:2–4: "I know a man in Christ, fourteen years ago (whether in the body,

I know not; or whether out of the body, I know not; God knoweth), such a one caught up even to the third heaven. And I know such a man (whether in the body, or apart from the body, I know not; God knoweth), how that he was caught up into Paradise, and heard unspeakable words, which it is not lawful for a man to utter."

Now you notice in those three passages the word *heaven* is used. It is used of three distinct—now, I am quite at a loss for the right word, and I always am so—spheres? regions? places? How shall we speak of the things that are beyond sense in terms that are wholly of the senses? But find your own word. You see what I mean.

First, Jesus uses the word *heaven* for the atmosphere surrounding the earth. Then we find, in the Acts of the Apostles, that the word is used of the vast stellar spaces that stretch away beyond the atmosphere—"wonders in the heaven above, and signs on the earth beneath." Then Paul, in the Corinthians, uses the term *the third heaven*. He declares that he knows a man who was caught up into that third heaven, who nevertheless came back again to solid earth. I do not waste any time arguing about that. Someone asked the other day if I really believed that. When I answered that most certainly I did, there was the question, "How did it happen?" Well, you don't expect me to know more than Paul did; he distinctly tells you that he does not know whether he was in the body or out of it. I have mentioned it to direct attention to a third heaven.

There are three heavens, then. But how they touch and merge is not the question. If we were discussing it speculatively—a foolish and dangerous thing—I might say that they all touch me at this moment. But if we like to think of them in sequence, there is, first, the atmosphere; second, the stellar spaces; and then, third, the heaven we speak of as the dwelling place of saint and seraphim—that place in the universe where God supremely manifests Himself to His worshipers, the third heaven.

Another word about this word *heaven*. The application is not yet patent, but we shall come back to it. We find this particular word (those familiar with the Greek Testament will at once recognize it) written sometimes in the singular number, and sometimes in the plural; that is one of the things which the translators have not always made clear. In all the instances I have read, the word is rendered in the singular; but you will find that the word is written in the plural when, Stephen being stoned, it is said of him that he saw the heavens opened. When it is plural you must, of course, decide by your context as to whether two or three heavens are referred to. When Peter speaks of the passing away of the heavens, he certainly means the first and the second, not the third. But when Stephen says, "I see the heavens opened," he certainly saw the whole of them opened. Those anointed eyes, baptized for suffering as well as for service, saw to the heart of the universe, to the very place where the light of God is supremely manifest. There, at the heart of the light, he saw the risen Christ.

But now, to come back to our word in this prayer—why have I taken all this time upon it? Because I want to indicate that in the invocation the word is plural, but in the qualifying phrase that ends the first three petitions the word is singular. So that, with perfect accuracy, Jesus taught us to pray, "Our Father who art in the heavens. Thy name be hallowed, Thy kingdom come, Thy will be done; as in heaven (singular), so on earth." Now, here I have two things which are to me of great value in my praying.

First, the incidental doctrine of God, with which Jesus introduces the prayer—the fact of His immanence and transcendence, the fact that God is in all heavens. Now, those of you who are following me with a new desire to pray already feel the tremendous force of the prayer: "Our Father, who art in all heavens." Where is He? In all heavens. Therefore, He is close to me as I pray; therefore, He is wherever that is for which I am praying.

But is this true? What about the first heaven? Jesus said, Not a sparrow shall fall on the ground—and oh, do not spoil great Scriptures by misquotation! Do not say, "Not a sparrow shall fall on the ground without your Father's knowledge"—blessed and true, but partial. He said not a sparrow "shall fall on the ground without your Father" (Matt. 10:29). God is with the sparrow as it falls. What about the stellar spaces? Because "He is strong in power, not one is lacking" (Isa. 40:26) these all are upheld. What about the far-distant places of saint and seraphim and light? No argument is needed, for this is God's supreme place of manifestation and dwelling. In all these, He is. Then, when I pray here, I know He is—

> Closer to me than breathing,
> Nearer than hands or feet.

But I know also that out yonder in China, India, and Africa He is. I know that is saying the nearest thing about Him. The stars in their courses fought *against* Sisera, but they fight *for* me; for God is the God of the second heaven as well as the God of the first. Out beyond I survey the infinite distances and wonder what enemy may lurk in them beyond my ken. That was what Paul was doing in Romans when he thought of the height and the depth. "Oh, no," he said, "God is for us—our Father, who art in all the heavens." The sigh of your need this morning, dear missionary, far from loved ones, takes in the whole tract of the universe and brings it into the service of your work. It seems to me that if we see this one thing, we shall pray as never before.

But now, what is the prayer itself? "As in heaven, so on earth." That is to say, I understand that when these men said, "Teach us to pray," and when, in the midst of the Manifesto Jesus corrected false methods of vain repetition—for that is what He was doing—"Use not vain repetitions, as the Gentiles do . . . but after this manner pray ye"—I understand He was teaching us that one of the first purposes of prayer is to ask that on this earth there should be set up the order that exists in that third and final heaven, which is without sin and without anything that is contradictory to the will of God. That is a broad statement, but surely it lies in the petition, "Hallowed be Thy name, Thy kingdom come, Thy will be done; as in heaven, so on earth." We are to pray for the setting up here of the heavenly order. Friends, that prayer will never be finally answered until we are gone. But it is our business today to pray for the final answer, and to pray for that new dispensation when the King Himself shall come and set up the rule of God upon the earth. But you may dismiss that if you like. Come back and see the passion of the prayer. Reverently, what does this mean? I think our mistake, very often, is to try and explain this ourselves. We are so unfamiliar with the third heaven, that we had better cease trying to do it. We had better come back to the one light and revelation if we are to understand the prayer that Jesus taught us.

Therefore, for one moment let us turn to the familiar word at the heart of the gospel of John, chapter 16 verse 28. You all know it. It is the key to the gospel: "I come out from the Father, and am come into the world: again, I leave the world, and go unto the Father." Now, there is the key to John, not only as to its analysis but as to its value. I am sure all of us will be agreed when I say that John has supremely shown us the fact of Christ as the Revealer. For instance, the word *heaven* never occurs in the gospel of John in the plural number; it is always singular. John's thought of heaven is always that third heaven.

Here Jesus is seen no longer as the King, as in Matthew; no longer as the Servant, as in Mark; no longer as the perfect Man, drawn by the hand of the Greek Luke. But here He is seen as the Word made flesh; that is, the speech of heaven made articulate for man's ear. "I come out from the Father," He said, "and am come into the world; again, I leave the world, and go unto the Father." But, when He came out from the Father, there came with Him the revelation of the order of the third heaven; and, in Him and through Him, I know what the order of the third heaven is. Now this, again, I think, can only be seen for purposes of intelligent prayer, as we attempt to grasp the whole outlook rather than the details. Take these writings of John. You all know the familiar words of John. You may arrange this gospel, or his first epistle, or the second, or the third, and, perhaps, the Apocalypse, around the selfsame three words, the simplest words of all in our language, and yet the sublimest—*love*, *light*, and *life*. Now, I do not hesitate to say that these three words reveal to us, in proportion as we hear them and understand them, all that we want to know of the order of the third heaven. I am sure you are agreed with me that it has been a great relief to think of heaven in some other way than the old one, with its harps, crowns, and robes. But it doesn't matter; the thing of supreme importance is the order, the method, the nature, the life.

Now, you see, I cannot explain this. I can only fling the words back upon you, the words you know. Jesus brought us these words—*love*, *light*, *life*. "Oh, but," you say, "we had them before." Friends, everything He said, we had before. He said nothing new, nothing absolutely new; He said everything new. You remember when He made the men's hearts burn within them on their way to Emmaus, it was not a new thing. Oh, this age of "new things"! It was their own Scriptures that He took and interpreted to them until the things that they knew best flamed with light and meaning. That was His whole mission: to take up the things that men had and to make them see them. Therefore, I repeat, He gave us these words. In the third heaven, love is the one and only and all-sufficient reason of activity. Whether it be God's revelation to those who worship, love is the reason of it. Whether it be the answering worship of those that behold, love is the impulse of it. Every note in the song of the seraphim and every beat of the wings of the cherubim is love impulsed. That is the third heaven. And light is the intelligence that lies along the pathway. When love drives, I walk in perfect intelligence. Light and life afford sufficient energy for walking in the light in answer to the impulse of love. That is heaven as Jesus revealed it—love, the impulse; light, the intelligence; life, the sufficient energy. Whenever I lift my eyes to that far-distant place and see it—not with eyes of sense, and hardly with faith, but always by revelation in some moment of waiting before God, that is the whole story—all they do is for love, all they do is in light, and all they do is in life.

Then we turn our eyes back to this earth of ours, and how different it all is! Here is the trouble with the world, look where you will upon it. Here is the thing that drives us out to evangelistic effort—that, whether at home or abroad, the story is not a story of love, not a story of light, not a story of life. It is not so yet, even to those who serve here. If love impulses, how often we blunder through lack of light! Even if love impulses, and we walk in the light, as yet, until the Advent morning, life is not sufficient to do all that love prompts! We all know what weariness is; if not, we are hardly Christian. No man in the ministry of Jesus Christ should ever put his head upon his pillow until he is tired out with toil. Any man or woman in the church who does not know what it is to share the travail that makes His kingdom come is dishonest and disloyal to Jesus Christ. What is weariness? It is the touch of death. Press that touch a little further, and all the weary wheels stand still. But *there* they never grow weary! Day and night, and "no light," perpetual, unceasing service; love driving, light flashing, life energizing—that is the third heaven.

Now, listen. Jesus said, "You want me to teach you to pray; pray for that, here, in this world." That came out of His sense of the world's need, sorrow, and sin. Pray that on this earth love may become the reason, light the intelligence, life the sufficient energy for the doing of the will of God. My friends, can that prayer be answered? How shall I answer my own question? By reminding you of the One who first taught us to pray this prayer nineteen centuries ago. Measuring God's goings by man's timetable seems a foolish thing to do. Nineteen centuries ago there stood in the midst of our world one Man who, for a generation, perchance, lived absolutely and wholly according to the order of the third heaven of God. Now, one would like to take a long time on that, but I need not—you know the story. Can you find anything in the life of Jesus that is not love-impulsed? He could be angry. One of the weaknesses of our age is that we imagine

He was soft, anemic—One who could not be angry. But if you had been a Pharisee robbing widows in those days, you would have known His anger, white-hot and scorching! But it was always love-impulsed, and that is where we fail. And light? He walked in light and never asked advice, never. He had no council, no committee. I hold that all my brethren in the succession of the apostles could not form a committee to advise Jesus. He did ask them something once when He said, "Whence are we to buy bread, that these may eat?" (John 6:5). All right, my brother; but wait a minute. What follows immediately in your Bible? "And this he said to prove him: for he himself knew what He would do" (v. 6). He walked in the light that fell straight out of the third heaven upon His pathway. He never hesitated, never faltered, never apologized. He walked in the light.

"Ah," you say, "but not in life." Yes, in life. How shall I put it? His dying was an act. Let His own word be the testimony about it: "No one taketh it [my life] away from me, but I lay it down of myself. I have power to lay it down, and I have power to take it again" (John 10:18). Sufficient energy to accomplish the will of God—that is the order of the third heaven. Whenever I pray that prayer now, I seem to hear the words coming from His dear lips, and I say, "Yes, He lived that!"

How did it all end? What did the world say to it all? You have only to lift your eyes, and you see Calvary. The world said, "We will not have this!" In the Cross hatred murdered love, darkness put out light, and men bound in death murdered the life-giver. Ah, but that is only one side! That is the side Peter had in mind when he said, "Ye by the hand of lawless men did crucify and slay . . ." (Acts 2:23b). But there is another side: "Him, being delivered up by the determinate counsel and foreknowledge of God . . ." (v. 23a). And we know—O Master, help me to say it—we know that when hatred murdered love, the very spear that pierced His side drew forth the blood to save! That is love's answer to man's hatred. We know that when men put Him, the light, out in the darkness, there streamed from the Cross the light (blessed be God!) in which we live and walk today. We know that when He was murdered, the mystery was met by the deeper, profounder mystery that He was laying down His life to take it again, to pass it to the men who, in their blindness and folly, had flung Him out. By that Cross this prayer can be answered.

For the moment, the church is the depository of all the forces that are to make for that kingdom. God has other methods, but I am not going to deal with them now. But when we pray our prayer, the first thing is passion for the coming of *His* kingdom. This is to be not so much for the world's sake—that, as it seems to me, is where our evangelical truth has weakened today—but for God's sake that God may win, that God may be vindicated, that He may get that upon which His heart is set. This is our prayer: "*Thy* name be hallowed, *Thy* kingdom come, *Thy* will be done. Thy name be hallowed in love, Thy kingdom come in light, Thy will be done in life—as in heaven, so here." May God, through Christ, "teach us to pray."

NOTES

Prayer: Adoration

David Martyn Lloyd-Jones (1898–1981) was born in Wales and was taken to London in 1914. There he trained for a medical career and was associated with the famous Dr. Thomas Horder in Harley Street. He abandoned medicine for the gospel ministry, and from 1927 to 1938 he served the Presbyterian Church at Sanfields, Aberavon, Wales. In 1938 he became associate minister with Dr. G. Campbell Morgan at the Westminster Chapel, London; and in 1943, when Morgan retired, Lloyd-Jones succeeded him. His expositions of the Scriptures attracted great crowds wherever he preached. He retired in 1968 to devote his time to writing and limited itinerant ministry. Calvinistic in doctrine, he emphasized the "plight of man and the power of God to save."

This message was reprinted from *Studies in the Sermon on the Mount,* volume 2, published in 1960 by William B. Eerdmans.

3

Prayer: Adoration

> After this manner therefore pray ye. Our Father which art in heaven, Hallowed by thy name. Thy kingdom come. Thy will be done in earth, as it is in heaven. (Matthew 6:9–10)

WE COME NOW to the next division of the Lord's Prayer, which is that which deals with our petitions. "Our Father which art in heaven," that is the invocation. Then come the petitions: "Hallowed be thy name. Thy kingdom come. Thy will be done in earth, as it is in heaven. Give us this day our daily bread. And forgive us our debts, as we forgive our debtors. And lead us not into temptation, but deliver us from evil." There has been much debating and disputing among the authorities as to whether there are six or seven petitions. The answer turns on whether that last statement "deliver us from evil" is to be regarded as a separate petition, or whether it is to be taken as part of the previous petition and to be read like this: "Lead us not into temptation but deliver us from evil." It is one of those points (and there are others in connection with the Christian faith) that simply cannot be decided, and about which we cannot be dogmatic. Fortunately for us, it is not a vital point, and God forbid that any of us should become so absorbed by the mere mechanics of Scripture and spend so much time with them as to miss the spirit and that which is important. The vital matter is not to decide whether there are six or seven petitions in the Lord's Prayer but rather to notice the order in which the petitions come. The first three—"Hallowed be thy name. Thy kingdom come. Thy will be done in earth, as it is in heaven"—have regard to God and His glory; the others have reference to ourselves. You will notice that the first three petitions contain the word *Thy*, and all have reference to God. It is only after that that the word *us* comes in: "Give us this day our daily bread. Forgive us our trespasses as we forgive those who trespass against us. Lead us not into temptation. Deliver us from evil." That is the vital point—the order of the petitions, not the number. The first three are concerned about and look only to God and His glory.

But let us observe something else which is of vital importance, the proportion in the petitions. Not only must our desires and petitions with regard to God come first, but we must notice, too, that half the petitions are devoted to God and His glory and only the rest deal with our particular needs and problems. Of course, if we are interested in biblical numerics—an interest that is perhaps not to be entirely discouraged, though it can become dangerous if and when we tend to become too fanciful—we shall see, in addition, that the first *three* petitions have reference to God, and that three is always the number of Deity and of God, suggesting the three blessed persons in the Trinity. In the same way, *four* is always the number of earth and refers to everything that is human. There are four beasts in the heavens in the book of Revelation, and so on. Seven, which is a combination of three and four, always stands for that perfect number where we see God in His relationship to earth and God in His dealing with men. That may be true of this prayer. Our Lord may have specifically constructed it to bring out those wonderful points. We cannot prove it. But, in any case, the important thing to grasp is this: it matters not what our conditions and circumstances may be, it matters not what our work may be, it matters not at all what our desires may be, we must never start with ourselves, we must never start with our own petitions.

That principle applies even when our petitions reach their highest level. Even our concern for the salvation of souls, even our concern for God's blessing upon the preaching of the Word, even our concern that those who are near and dear to us may become truly Christian, even these things must never be given the first place, the first position. Still less must we ever start with our own circumstances and conditions.

It does not matter how desperate they may be; it does not matter how acute the tension; it does not matter whether it be physical illness, war, a calamity, or some terrible problem suddenly confronting us: whatever it may be, we must never fail to observe the order that is taught here by our blessed Lord and Savior. Before we begin to think of ourselves and our own needs, even before our concern for others, we must start with this great concern about God and His honor and His glory. There is no principle in connection with the Christian life that exceeds this in importance. So often we err in the realm of principles. We tend to assume that we are quite sound and clear about principles, and that all we need is instruction about details. The actual truth, of course, is the exact reverse of that. If only we would always start in prayer with this true sense of the invocation. If only we were to recollect that we are in the presence of God and that the eternal and almighty God is there, looking upon us as our Father and more ready to bless and to surround us with His love than we are to receive His blessing, we should achieve more in that moment of recollection than all our prayers put together are likely to achieve without that realization. If only we all had this concern about God and His honor and glory!

Fortunately, our Lord knows our weakness, He realizes our need of instruction, so He has divided it up for us. He has not only announced the principle, but He has divided it up for us into these three sections which we must proceed to consider. Let us look now at the first petition: "Hallowed be thy name."

Hallowed Be Thy Name

We realize now that we are in the presence of God and that He is our Father. Therefore this, says Christ, should be our first desire, our first petition: "Hallowed be thy name." What does that mean? Let us look very briefly at the words. The word *hallowed* means "to sanctify, to revere, or to make and keep holy." But why does He say "Hallowed be thy name"? What does this term the *name* stand for? We are familiar with the fact that it was the way in which the Jews at that time commonly referred to God Himself. Whatever we may say about the Jews in Old Testament times and however great their failures, there was one respect, at any rate, in which they were most commendable. I refer to their sense of the greatness and the majesty and the holiness of God. You remember that they had such a sense of this that it had become their custom not to use the name *Jehovah*. They thought that the very name, the very letters, as it were, were so holy and sacred, and they so small and unworthy, that they dare not mention it. They referred to God as "The Name" to avoid the use of the actual term *Jehovah*. So that the *name* here means God Himself. We see that the purpose of the petition is to express this desire that God Himself may be revered, may be sanctified, that the very name of God and all it denotes and represents may be honored among men, may be holy throughout the entire world. But perhaps in the light of the Old Testament teaching it is good for us to enlarge on this just a little. The *name,* in other words, means all that is true of God and all that has been revealed concerning God. It means God in all His attributes, God in all that He is in and of Himself, and God in all that He has done and all that He is doing.

God, you remember, had revealed Himself to the children of Israel under various names. He had used a term concerning Himself *(El* or *Elohim)* that means His "strength" and His "power." When He used that particular name, He was giving the people a sense of His might, His dominion, and His power. Later, He revealed Himself in that great and wonderful name

Jehovah, which really means "the self-existent One," "I am that I am," eternally self-existent. But there were other names in which God described Himself: "the Lord will provide" (*Jehovah-jireh*), "the Lord that healeth" (*Jehovah-rapha*), "the Lord our Banner" (*Jehovah-nissi*), "the Lord our peace" (*Jehovah-Shalom*), "the Lord our Shepherd" (*Jehovah-ra-ah*), "the Lord our Righteousness" (*Jehovah-tsidkenu*), and another term which means, "the Lord is present" (*Jehovah-shammah*). As you read the Old Testament, you will find all of these various terms used. In giving these various names to Himself, God was revealing Himself and something of His nature and being, His character and His attributes to mankind. In a sense, "thy name" stands for all that. Our Lord is here teaching us to pray that the whole world may come to know God in this way, that the whole world may come to honor God like that. It is the expression of a burning and deep desire for the honor and glory of God.

You cannot read the four Gospels without seeing very clearly that that was the consuming passion of the Lord Jesus Christ Himself. It is found again perfectly in that great High Priestly prayer in John 17 when He says, "I have glorified thee on the earth" (v. 4), and "I have manifested thy name unto the men which thou gavest me" (v. 6). He was always concerned about the glory of His Father. He said, "I seek not mine own glory: there is one that seeketh and judgeth" (8:50). There is no real understanding of the earthly life of Christ except in these terms. He knew that glory which ever belongs to the Father, "the glory which I had with thee before the world was" (17:5). He had seen that glory, and He had shared it. He was filled with this sense of the glory of God, and His one desire was that mankind might come to know it.

What unworthy ideas and notions this world has of God! If you test your ideas of God by the teaching of the Scriptures, you will see at a glance what I mean. We lack even a due sense of the greatness and the might and the majesty of God. Listen to men arguing about God and notice how glibly they use the term. It is not that I would advocate a return to the practice of

the ancient Jews. I think they went too far. But it is indeed almost alarming to observe the way in which we all tend to use
the name of God. We obviously do not realize that we are
talking about the ever blessed, eternal, and absolute, almighty
God. There is a sense in which we should take our shoes off
our feet whenever we use the name. And how little do we appreciate the goodness of God, the kindness and the providence
of God. How the psalmist delighted in celebrating God as our
rock, God as our peace, God as our shepherd who leads us,
God as our righteousness, and God as the ever present One
who will never leave us nor forsake us.

This petition means just that. We should all have a consuming passion that the whole world might come to know God like
that. There is an interesting expression used in the Old Testament with regard to this which must sometimes have aston-
ished us. The psalmist in Psalm 34 invites everybody to join
him in "magnifying" the Lord. What a strange idea! "O," he
says, "magnify the LORD with me, and let us exalt his name together" (v. 3). At first sight, that appears to be quite ridiculous. God is the Eternal, the self-existent One, absolute and
perfect in all His qualities. How can feeble man ever magnify
such a Being? How can we ever make God great or greater
(which is what we mean by magnify)? How can we exalt the
name that is highly exalted over all? It seems preposterous and
quite ridiculous. And yet, of course, if we but realize the way
in which the psalmist uses it, we shall see exactly what he means.
He does not mean that we can *actually* add to the greatness of
God, for that is impossible. But he does mean that he is concerned that this greatness of God may appear to be greater
among men. Thus it comes to pass that among ourselves in
this world we can magnify the name of God. We can do so by
words, and by our lives, by being reflectors of the greatness
and the glory of God and of His glorious attributes.

That is the meaning of this petition. It means a burning desire that the whole world may bow before God in adoration, in
reverence, in praise, in worship, in honor, and in thanksgiving.

Is that our supreme desire? Is that the thing that is always up-permost in our minds whenever we pray to God? I would re-mind you again that it should be so whatever our circumstances. It is when we look at it in that way that we see how utterly value-less much of our praying must be. When you come to God, says our Lord, in effect, even though you may be in desperate condi-tions and circumstances, it may be with some great concern on your mind and in your heart. Even then, He says, stop for a moment and just recollect and realize that your greatest desire of all should be that this wonderful God, who has become your Father in and through Me, should be honored, worshiped, and magnified among the people. "Hallowed be thy name." And as we have seen, it has always been so in the praying of every true saint of God that has ever lived on the face of the earth.

If, therefore, we are anxious to know God's blessing and are concerned that our prayers should be effectual and of value, we must follow this order. It is all put in a phrase repeated many times in the Old Testament: "The fear of the Lord is the beginning of wisdom." That is the conclusion reached by the psalmist. That is the conclusion, likewise, of the wise man in his proverbs. If you want to know, he says, what true wisdom is, if you want to be blessed and prosperous, if you want to have peace and joy, if you want to be able to live and die in a worthy manner, if you want wisdom with regard to life in this world, here it is: "the fear of the Lord." That does not mean craven fear; it means reverential awe. If, therefore, we want to know God and to be blessed of God, we must start by worship-ing Him. We must say, "Hallowed be thy name," and tell Him that, before mentioning any concern about ourselves, our one desire is that He shall be known. Let us approach God "with reverence and godly fear: for our God is a consuming fire" (Heb. 12:28–29). That is the first petition.

The Kingdom Come

The second is "Thy kingdom come." You notice that there is a logical order in these petitions. They follow one another by a kind of inevitable, divine necessity. We began by asking that the name of God may be hallowed among men. But the moment we pray that prayer we are reminded of the fact that His name is not hallowed thus. At once the question arises, Why do not all men bow before the sacred name? Why is not every man on this earth concerned about humbling himself now in the presence of God, and worshiping Him and using every moment in adoring Him and spreading forth His name? Why not? The answer is, of course, because of sin, because there is another kingdom, the kingdom of Satan, the kingdom of darkness. And there, at once, we are reminded of the very essence of the human problems and the human predicament.

Our desire as Christian people is that God's name shall be glorified. But the moment we start with that we realize that there is this opposition, and we are reminded of the whole biblical teaching about evil. There is another who is "the god of this world." There is a kingdom of darkness, a kingdom of evil, and it is opposed to God and His glory and honor. But God has been graciously pleased to reveal from the very dawn of history that He is yet going to establish His kingdom in this world of time. Even though Satan has entered in and conquered the world for the time being and the whole of mankind is under his dominion, God is again going to assert Himself and turn this world and all its kingdoms into His own glorious kingdom.

In other words, running right through the Old Testament, there are the promises and the prophecies concerning the coming of the kingdom of God or the kingdom of heaven. And, of course, at this particular, crucial point of world history, when our Lord Himself was here on earth, this matter was very much in the forefront of men's minds. John the Baptist had been preaching his message, "Repent ye: for the kingdom of heaven is at hand" (Matt. 3:2). He called the people to be ready for it. And when our Lord began preaching, He said exactly the same thing: "Repent: for the kingdom of heaven is at hand" (4:17). In this petition, He obviously has that whole idea in His mind as He teaches His disciples to offer this particular prayer. At that immediate historical point, He was teaching His disciples to pray that this kingdom of God would come increasingly and come quickly. But the prayer is equally true and equally right for us as Christian people in all ages until the end shall come.

We can summarize the teaching concerning the kingdom. The kingdom of God really means the reign of God; it means the law and the rule of God. When we look at it like that we can see that the kingdom can be regarded in three ways. In one sense, the kingdom has already come. It came when the Lord Jesus Christ was here. He said, "If I with the finger of God cast out devils, no doubt the kingdom of God is come upon you" (Luke 11:20). He said in effect, "The kingdom of God is here now; I am exercising this power, this sovereignty, this majesty, this dominion. This is the kingdom of God." So the kingdom of God in one sense had come then. The kingdom of God is also here at this moment in the hearts and lives of all who submit to Him, in all who believe in Him. The kingdom of God is present in the church, in the heart of all those who are truly Christian. Christ reigns in such people. But the day is yet to come when His kingdom shall have been established here upon the earth. The day is yet to come when

> Jesus shall reign where'er the sun
> Does his successive journeys run.

That day is coming. The whole message of the Bible looks forward to that. Christ came down from heaven to earth to found, to establish, and to bring in this kingdom. He is still engaged upon that task and will be until the end, when it shall have been completed. Then He will, according to Paul, hand it back to God the Father, "that God may be all in all" (1 Cor. 15:28).

So our petition really amounts to this. We should have a great longing and desire that the kingdom of God and of Christ may come in the hearts of men. It should be our desire that this kingdom should be extended in our own hearts. For it is to the extent that we worship Him and surrender our lives to Him and are led by Him that His kingdom comes in our hearts. We should also be anxious to see this kingdom extending in the lives and hearts of other men and women. So that when we pray, "Thy kingdom come," we are praying for the success of the gospel, its sway and power. We are praying for the conversion of men and women. We are praying that the kingdom of God may come today in Britain, in Europe, in America, in Australia, everywhere in the world. "Thy kingdom come" is an all-inclusive missionary prayer.

But it goes even further than that. It is a prayer that indicates that we are "Looking for and hasting unto the coming of the day of God" (2 Peter 3:12). It means that we should be anticipating the day when all sin and evil and wrong and everything that is opposed to God shall finally have been routed. It means that we should have longings in our hearts for the time when the Lord will come back again, when all that is opposed to Him shall be cast into the lake of burning, and the kingdoms of this world shall have become the kingdoms of our God and of His Christ.

> Thy kingdom come, O God;
> Thy rule, O Christ, begin;
> Break with Thine iron rod
> The tyrannies of sin.

That is the petition. Indeed its meaning is expressed perfectly at the very end of the book of Revelation. "Even so, come, Lord Jesus" (22:20). "The Spirit and the bride say, Come" (v. 17). Our Lord is just emphasizing here that before we begin to think of our own personal needs and desires, we should have this burning desire within us for the coming of His kingdom that the name of God may be glorified and magnified over all.

Thy Will Be Done in Earth, as It Is in Heaven

The third petition—"Thy will be done in earth, as it is in heaven"—needs no explanation. It is a kind of logical consequence and conclusion from the second, as that was a logical conclusion from the first. The result of the coming of the kingdom of God among men will be that the will of God will be done among men. In heaven, the will of God is always being done perfectly. We have only some dim and faint figures of it in the Scriptures, but we have sufficient to know that what is characteristic of heaven is that everyone and everything is waiting upon God and anxious to glorify and magnify His name. The angels, as it were, are on the wing all ready and waiting to fly at His bidding. The supreme desire of all in heaven is to do the will of God, and thereby to praise and worship Him. And it should be the desire of every true Christian, says our Lord here, that all on earth should be the same. Here, again, we are looking forward to the coming of the kingdom because this petition will never be fulfilled and granted until the kingdom of God shall indeed be established here on earth among men. Then the will of God will be done on earth as it is done in heaven. There will be "new heavens and a new earth, wherein dwelleth righteousness" (2 Peter 3:13). Heaven and earth will become one, the world will be changed, evil will be burned out of it, and the glory of God will shine over all.

In these words, then, we are taught how we begin to pray. Those are the petitions with which we must always start. We can summarize them again in this way. Our innermost and greatest desire should be the desire for God's honor and glory. At the risk of being misunderstood, I suggest that our desire for this should be even greater than our desire for the salvation of souls. Before we even begin to pray for souls, before we even begin to pray for the extension and the spread of God's kingdom, there should be that overruling desire for the manifestation of the glory of God and that all might humble themselves in His presence. We can put it like this. What is it that troubles and worries our minds? Is it the manifestation of sin that we see in the world, or is it the fact that men do not worship and glorify God as they ought to do? Our Lord felt it so much that He put it like this in John 17:25: "O righteous

Father, the world hath not known thee: but I have known thee, and these [referring to the disciples] have known that thou hast sent me." "Righteous Father," He said in effect, "Here is the tragedy, here is the thing that perplexes Me and saddens Me, that the world has not known You. It thinks of You as a tyrant. It thinks of You as a harsh Lawgiver. It thinks of You as Someone who is opposed to it and always tyrannizing over it. Holy Father, the world has not known You. If it had but known You, it could never think of You like that." And that should be our attitude, that should be our burning desire and longing. We should so know God that our one longing and desire should be that the whole world should come to know Him too.

What a wonderful prayer this is. O the folly of people who say that such a prayer is not meant for Christians, but that it was meant only for the disciples then and for the Jews in some coming age. Does it not make us feel in a sense that we have never prayed at all? This is prayer. "Our Father which art in heaven, Hallowed be thy name." Have we arrived at that yet, I wonder? Have we really prayed that prayer, that petition, "Hallowed be thy name"? If only we are right about that, the rest will follow. "Thy kingdom come. Thy will be done in earth, as it is in heaven." We need not turn to Him and ask Him, "Lord, teach us how to pray." He has done so already. We have but to put into practice the principles He has taught us so plainly in this model prayer.

NOTES

The Lord's Prayer

John A. Broadus (1827–1895) has long been recognized as the "Dean of American teachers of homiletics." His work *The Preparation and Delivery of Sermons,* in its many revisions, has been a basic textbook for preachers since it was first published in 1870. Born and educated in Virginia, Broadus pastored the Baptist church at Charlottesville, and in 1859 became Professor of New Testament Interpretation and of Homiletics at the Southern Baptist Theological Seminary. He was named president of the school in 1888.

This sermon was taken from *Favorite Sermons of John A. Broadus,* published by Harper Brothers, 1959.

4

The Lord's Prayer

Our Father which art in heaven, Hallowed be thy name.
(Matthew 6:9)

THE PRAYER THAT THUS BEGINS, that for many ages has been called among Christians "the Lord's Prayer," is above all eulogies for its sweetness. No wonder this is so! For our Lord presents it as a specimen, as a model of prayer. He said, "When ye pray, use not vain repetitions, as the heathen do: for they think that they shall be heard for their much speaking" (Matt. 6:7), saying over the same thing a thousand times. "Be ye not therefore like unto them: for your Father knoweth what things ye have need of, before ye ask him" (v. 8). *Thus* then do *you* pray—this way and not with vain repetitions, not with much speaking, *thus* do you pray! He gives it as a sample, as a model. So on a later occasion, recorded in the eleventh chapter of Luke—probably a long time after this, most likely in quite another part of the country, certainly on a later occasion—our Lord was praying Himself. When He ceased, the disciples asked Him, "Teach us to pray," and He said, "When ye pray, say . . ." Then He gave them substantially the same prayer as the one here before us.

Now it very naturally occurs to many persons that our Lord has given this as a *form* of prayer, that when we pray we ought always to say these words. I do not object to using these words whenever anyone thinks them appropriate, that they express his sentiments, but it is very certain that our Lord did not give this as a form of prayer. If you will notice a moment I shall prove it. On the second occasion, the prayer is very different from that which we here read. Even in the common text, it is different in several expressions. But if you will take any revised text as furnished by any competent scholar of the day, you will find that the prayer on that occasion is quite different. Allow me to repeat it as it is there. You all know the words as they occur here. But on that second occasion this is what He said: "Father, hallowed be thy name. Thy kingdom come. Give us day by day our daily bread. And forgive us our sins; for we ourselves also forgive every one that is indebted to us. And bring us not into temptation" (Luke 11:2–4 ASV).

Now you observe that I have omitted several phrases of the familiar prayer given here in the Sermon on the Mount. If you look a little closely you notice that nothing of essential importance, no distinctive idea, has been omitted here. Instead of "Our Father which art in heaven," you have simply "Father." You have lost some pleasing words, but you have really lost no part of the essential thought. When after the petition "Thy kingdom come" you find wanting the words "Thy will be done on earth as it is in heaven," you observe in a moment that although a pleasing expression has been expunged, it is involved in the preceding petition, "Thy kingdom come." For when God's reign on earth is fully come, His will must of necessity be done on earth as in heaven. And so, when after the prayer "Bring us not into temptation" you miss the words "But deliver us from evil," you observe that they do, at most, but express the other side of the same truth—something that is implied in the words that remain.

On that second occasion then, our Lord has omitted no idea that belongs to the prayer. It is substantially the very same, but in form it is exceedingly different. Is not there the proof at once that he did not intend this as a form of prayer? If He did so intend, why in the world should He not have repeated His form correctly on the second occasion? No, He intended it not as a form of prayer, that precisely these words should be used, but as an example, "Thus do ye pray." Avoid the vain repetitions and much speaking of the heathen. Thus, thus comprehensively, thus simply. Oh, how much is included in these few, brief, simply expressed petitions! "Thus then do ye pray."

And my brethren, I venture to ask your special attention to this model in one respect. We have two good classes of petitions here, as is obvious at once, petitions with reference to God's glory, and petitions with reference to our own good. And my point is that the petitions with reference to God's glory come first. Now you have noticed, and indeed it seems natural to us that when we pray, we pray first about ourselves and a great deal about ourselves. Then if we do not forget, if there seems to be time left before we close the prayer, we may introduce some petitions as to God's glory. But here the class of petitions that refer to God's glory come first. That is their rightful place. I do not feel they should always come first in order, that there ought to be any formality or stiffness in it, but that they should often be put in the place of priority and regularly in the place of preeminence. Much more important is it that God's name should be hallowed and God's kingdom come in the world, than that you and I, as individuals, should gain the blessings we desire.

And now I propose to you, that while we cannot bring out many of the thoughts involved in this comprehensive prayer, we shall try to get some practical lessons from it.

Petitions That Relate to God's Glory

"Hallowed be thy name." The words are so simple, we have known them so well from our childhood that it is really difficult to stop and ask what they mean. Let Your name be made holy. God's name represents Himself. It is a prayer that His name, and Himself as represented by His name, may be regarded as holy—spoken of as holy—treated as holy. We have a model here in the picture given by Isaiah, the adoring seraphs covering their faces in awe before the throne. What do they cry? Not, as often we do; great, majestic, glorious—not a word about His power, nor even about His wisdom—"Holy, Holy, Holy, Lord God of Hosts." That is the central thought that ought to be our deepest desire, that God may be regarded and spoken of and treated as *holy*.

Oh, what a contrast between that scene of the vision, and the sights and the souls of this world in which we live. Walk the streets anywhere. Listen to the talk wherever you find it, especially when men grow excited. Hear them! Hear how that high and holy name is bandied as a jest and polluted with profanity. It is enough to make a man shiver to hear the profanity that abounds everywhere. I have shivered, literally, sometimes as I listened.

But my friends, have we nothing to do but to look with horror at other men's profanity? There are some things important to our own life here. Have a care that while you may not use in vain the sacred name of God itself, you shall not fall into the practice of using other sacred expressions lightly and irreverently. I have heard even refined ladies use phrases in a light way that were appropriate only in solemn prayer, and to a certain extent that was irreverence, that was profanity. Have a care about indulging wit that comes from profaning the language of Scripture and allusions to God. Bluff old Dr. Johnson once said that "a man that has any respect for himself ought to be above that kind of wit, it is so cheap: any one can do that." Yes, anyone that has any respect for himself ought to be above that kind of wit, and a man that has any reverence for God ought to shrink from it. Have a care how you repeat the profanity of other men. You want to tell a good story and the point of it perhaps lies in a profane expression. Now should you repeat that expression? Is it good for yourself to repeat it? Is it healthy? Especially is it good for that boy there that is hearing and may not make the nice distinction that you make, when you repeat other men's profanity? I would not inculcate scrupulosity about trifles. But perchance this is not a trifle, it seems to me that we who pray this prayer ought to lay such things to our hearts, and shrink with horror and cultivate ourselves into shrinking with shuddering from anything like profanity. Oh, that God's name might always be spoken with deepest reverence. Oh, that God Himself might come to be everywhere thought of, and talked about, and obeyed, as holy. Anyhow, let us try to have it so in our hearts, on our lips, in our lives.

And the second petition, "Thy reign come." I am not going to explain all these simple words, of course, but here is one that wants explaining. The Greek word which is rendered "kingdom" in the text requires three English words to convey its meaning. Primarily the word means "kingship," the condition of being a king, the possession of royal power. Then secondarily it means "reign," the exercise of royal power. As a final derivation it means what we call "kingdom," subjects or territory over whom or in which this royal power is exercised. Kingship, and reign, and kingdom. There are many cases of that kind in translation, where several terms have to be used in one language to convey the meaning of a single word in another. Now the leading thought here is evidently that which we express by the word "reign." And the reference is to the messianic reign that the prophets had long foretold, that messianic reign of which David had sung, that messianic reign that John the Baptist had declared was now near at hand. Jesus at the beginning of His ministry in Galilee took up the same cry, "The kingdom of God is at hand: repent ye, and believe the gospel" (Mark 1:15). Men had long prayed that that reign might come, and now there was all the more propriety in such a prayer, for it was near at hand.

Do you think there is no need of that prayer still? Do you think the reign, the messianic reign of God in the world, has come? It has but begun. It was beginning when Jesus taught these teachings. It began still more when He rose triumphant from the grave and ascended glorious into the sky. It began still further on the day of Pentecost. It began in another sense at the destruction of Jerusalem, which He spoke of beforehand as the time when He should come in His kingdom. It has begun on the earth, ah! it has not come yet. Alas, for the wide portions of the world where the very name of the King Messiah has not come. Alas, in the metropolis of one of the great Christian nations of today, the great mass of the men that surge around us, are utterly unsanctified by the gospel, utterly heedless of the reign of God. Stop any moment and think, between two heartbeats, of this great world you live in, of this great city you live in, and then you shall address yourself with new fervor to the prayer: "Thy reign come, O God! thy reign!" Anyhow, let it come in us. Let it pervade our whole being. Let it control our whole life. Let it sanctify our home life. Let it elevate our social life. Let it purify our business life. Let men feel, as they note our conduct, that we are subjects of the Lord God.

I shall not dwell, for lack of time, upon the third petition here, which is but an expansion of the preceding. For, as I have said, whenever God's reign has fully come, then His will must be done on earth. Many things occur now that are not according to God's will. The prayer is that God's will may take place and that everything may happen on earth in accordance with God's will, as in heaven everything does happen. Many times for us, I know it is hard even to *consent* that this shall be so. When it is plainly God's will that something should happen, which to us is painful, we shrink and with difficulty we say, "Thy will be done." No wonder, it has been so with better persons than we are. Certain disciples, when they besought Paul not to go up to Jerusalem and he would not be persuaded, ceased and said, "The will of the Lord be done." The struggling Savior in Gethsemane, as He strove in agony and prayer to nerve Himself for what He had to bear, said again and again—for it would not stay said: "Nevertheless not my will, but thine, be done" (Luke 22:42). No wonder we find it hard sometimes to say that. The prayer teaches us not merely to submit to God's will, but to desire that God's will may take place in the world. To desire that everything concerning us and concerning all around us may happen according to His will. And if He takes away our property, our health, our usefulness, our life, or someone we love better than our life, still we would say and we should rejoice when we say, "Thy will be done." Oh, if it could be so. If in the world, whether gaining or losing, in success or failure, it could be so in us and about us that God's will were done in all things—what a joy in the thought. What a springing gladness it puts into the heart, the very idea!

Petitions That Relate to Ourselves

But perhaps we shall find not more important but more practical lessons if we turn to the second part of the prayer—petitions relating to ourselves.

"Give us this day our daily bread." Now I entreat you, don't listen to the commentaries, so many of which tell you that this means spiritual bread. I am weary of that everlasting spiritualizing. Spiritual things are far above temporal things, but there are many references in the Scriptures to our temporal and material wants. Why should we lose their meaning and sustaining power because we go on allegorizing everything? It is plainly a prayer for temporal good as represented by that which is most essential and thus stated in the simplest possible form, and a prayer with reference simply to day after day. A little child sees its meaning and feels its sweetness, and the wisest man can find no higher wisdom than to cry still, "Give us this day our daily bread."

My friends, I should be inclined to think that above all the petitions of the prayer this needs to be enforced in our time. I have known some Christians who were very unwilling to realize that there was any human exertion in obtaining spiritual good. They say, if that be true, how is it the gift of God? And if it be the gift of God, how can it be the effort of our own labor? Yet if spiritual good is the gift of God, so is temporal good the gift of God, though it is obtained only by human effort. The truth is, we see, that both are the gift of God, and both are the result of our own exertions.

Especially with reference to one of the great tendencies of thought in our time is it important that we should cherish this petition for our daily bread. "Pshaw!" men say, "that depends upon physical forces and laws, upon material things, upon your own exertion, upon the climate and the weather." Now in the face of these notions it becomes all the more appropriate that we should pray to God to give us daily bread. Yes, and I tell you plainly and boldly, though I have not time to develop the thought, if it is not right and wise to ask God for daily bread, if as they tell you in the newspapers so often, there is no efficacy in prayer, there is no use in praying for rain, then there is no God at all. You are driven straight to it by absolute logical necessity. If it is not proper to pray for daily bread and to pray for rain, there is no God. There is nothing in existence but matter with its organization and its results. You cannot help it. There is no standing room, for the life of you, between those two positions. Alas, alas, how many in our time, one-sided or superficial, have gone into utter materialism. Never was there a time when it was more needful that the Christian world should realize in their experience the sentiment of this prayer. We work for daily bread and plan for years to come, but nonetheless are we to seek it as the daily gift of the daily goodness of our Father in heaven.

"And forgive us our debts, as we forgive our debtors." The simple prayer for temporal things all embraced in that one petition for what is most indispensable, and now in addition, a twofold prayer—forgiveness for past sin and deliverance from sin in the future. That our God may be glorified, that our earthly wants may be supplied, and that we may be forgiven our sin and delivered from evil—that is all there is to pray for.

You know that the term *debt* is used here as an Aramaic expression to denote sin—sin regarded as a debt, which we must pay to God, or in the kindred phrase of other languages, "pay the penalty." You notice that when our Lord repeats the thought a moment later He says *trespasses*, or transgressions. ou remember that when He gives the prayer on a subsequent occasion it is "Forgive us our sins; for we ourselves also forgive every one that is indebted to us" (Luke 11:4). "Forgive us our debts" means forgive us our sins. My friends, does it ever occur to you that you are more anxious about the "give" than the "forgive"? Does it ever happen in your experience that you pray that God would give and forget to ask that God would forgive? And yet, is not this last as deep a need? Yes, a deeper need than the other? Ah! that a man should have all earthly things given him, and his sins not forgiven, would be a poor gift. Yet a man who should be deprived of all earthly things and go starving into the other world, yet with his sins forgiven, would be rich and might rejoice. Let us not forget as we go on praying for what God has to give, to ask still more earnestly that He would forgive us our sins.

I must beg you in connection with the prayer to dwell upon the condition that our Lord here presents. It is a matter of the utmost practical importance to all of us. "Forgive us our debts, as we forgive our debtors." You have noticed surely that after completing this simple prayer Jesus before going on to speak of other things, takes up again one of the thoughts of the prayer. Which one is it? Something about God's name being hallowed or His reign coming? Something about daily bread? Something about temptation or evil? No, it is this one. This one thought He repeats, repeats it positively and negatively. For if you forgive men their trespasses, your heavenly Father will also forgive you, and if you forgive not, neither will your heavenly Father forgive you. You know why—you know yourself but little if you do not well know why He dwells upon this. The disposition to be revengeful, or at any rate to be unforgiving, is one of the deepest rooted, one of the hardest to correct, one of the most hurtful and ruinous in its influence, of all the evil dispositions that belong to our sinful human nature. So our Lord presents forgiving as the condition of being forgiven, the condition *sine qua non*—if we do not forgive men, we cannot be forgiven. He does not mean that our forgiving is the meritorious ground of our being forgiven. It is an indispensable condition. Only if we do forgive men can we be forgiven, but

then we are forgiven on the ground that the gospel provides—
the merit that is not our own.

Now let us make a practical distinction. We use that word
forgive in a somewhat ambiguous fashion. In the strict and
proper sense it is not our duty to forgive a man unless he repents. God forgives in that sense no man but the penitent. Jesus
said, you remember, "If he [your brother] trespass against thee
seven times in a day, and seven times in a day turn . . . saying,
I repent; thou shalt forgive him" (Luke 17:4). It is not right
that you should restore a man to the confidence he has for-
feited unless he shows himself worthy of it. It is not right that
you should forgive a man, in the full sense of the term, unless
he repents. Not only is it not your duty, but it is not right. "Love
your enemies . . . that ye may be the children of your Father
which is in heaven" (Matt. 5:44–45a). God forgives only the
penitent and loves them as His friends, but even the impenitent God loves. "He maketh his sun to rise on the evil and on
the good, and sendeth rain on the just and on the unjust" (v.
45b). He wishes His enemies no harm but does them good.
We need not, and really should not, forgive a man in the full
sense while he remains impenitent, but we must in the other
sense forgive him. We must bear him no malice. We must do
him no harm. We must be glad to do him good in anything
that will not promote his evil designs against us. Thus shall we
be the sons of our Father in heaven.

I think this distinction is practically important. The idea of
forgiving a man who is impenitent does seem to be impracti-
cable, and that is not what the Scriptures teach. But that we
should bear no malice and yield to no revenge, that is what
the Scriptures teach. Ah me, even this is hard enough for poor
human nature! Let us strive to do that. Let us lay it to heart.
Who is there here today among us who has not sometimes
thought himself to have been cruelly wronged? Who? We all
have need then to exercise this forgiveness.

And finally, "bring us not into temptation." For it is not simply *lead*, it is *bring*. Human agency is, for the moment, here

left out of account. The thought is of God's providence as bearing us on and bringing us into certain situations, and the prayer is that God will not bring us into circumstances of temptation of trial. Why? Because we are afraid we cannot stand temptation. Ah, every man that knows himself will most certainly feel an echo in his heart, "I am weak, O Lord, bring me not into temptation."

A man advertised for a coachman, and when the applicants came he asked each one, "How near would you undertake to run my carriage wheel to the edge of a precipice?" The first one said he would run within a foot of it. The second said he would run within six inches. The third was an Irishman who said, "I would kape away as far as I could," and he got the place. Maybe you will remember that if you forget my solemn injunction. O my Christian friends, pray that you may be kept away from temptation for you are weak, and let him that thinks he stands take heed lest he fall.

"Bring us not into temptation, but deliver us from evil." This simple prayer ought as a model to control all our praying. Its spirit ought to strike into our blood, shaping our whole character, regulating our whole life. And as we pray it, oh, ought not our life's endeavor to accord with it? What folly to pray, "Thy reign come," and never a finger lifted to urge forward the progress of that reign—never a sacrifice made, never a deed done, never a word spoken, nothing but idle prayer. What folly to pray for forgiveness of sin and pray for deliverance from evil if along with the prayer there be not the cherished desire after holiness and the perpetual effort to abhor—to *abhor*—that which is evil and cleave to that which is good.

The Fatherhood of God

Charles Haddon Spurgeon (1834–1892) is undoubtedly the most famous minister of the nineteenth century. Converted in 1850, he united with the Baptists and soon began to preach in various places. He became pastor of the Baptist church in Waterbeach, England, in 1851, and three years later he was called to the decaying Park Street Church, London. Within a short time, the work began to prosper, a new church was built and dedicated in 1861, and Spurgeon became London's most popular preacher. In 1855 he began to publish his sermons weekly; today they make up the fifty-seven volumes of *The Metropolitan Tabernacle Pulpit*. He founded a pastor's college and several orphanages.

This sermon was taken from *The New Park Street Pulpit,* volume 4.

5

The Fatherhood of God

Our Father which art in heaven. (Matthew 6:9)

I THINK THERE IS ROOM for very great doubt whether our Savior intended the prayer, of which our text forms a part, to be used in the manner in which it is commonly employed among professing Christians. It is the custom of many persons to repeat it as their morning prayer, and they think that when they have repeated these sacred words they have done enough. I believe that this prayer was never intended for universal use. Jesus Christ taught it not to all men, but to His disciples, and it is a prayer adapted only to those who are the possessors of grace and are truly converted. In the lips of an ungodly man it is entirely out of place. Does not one say, "You are of your father the devil, for his works you do?" (see John 8:44). Why, then, should ye mock God by saying, "Our Father which art in heaven." For how can He be your Father? Have you two Fathers? And if He be a Father, where is His honor? Where is His love? You neither honor nor love Him. Yet you presumptuously and blasphemously approach Him and say, "Our Father," when your heart is attached still to sin and your life is opposed to His law, and you therefore prove yourself to be an heir of wrath and not a child of grace! Oh! I beseech you, leave

off sacrilegiously employing these sacred words. Until you can
in sincerity and truth say, "Our Father which art in heaven,"
and in your lives seek to honor His holy name, do not offer to
Him the language of the hypocrite, which is an abomination
to Him.

I very much question also whether this prayer was intended
to be used by Christ's own disciples as a constant form of prayer.
It seems to me that Christ gave it as a model whereby we are
to fashion all our prayers. I think we may use it to edification,
and with great sincerity and earnestness, at certain times and
seasons. I have seen an architect form the model of a building
he intends to erect of plaster or wood, but I never had an idea
that it was intended for me to live in. I have seen an artist trace
on a piece of brown paper, perhaps, a design that he intended
afterward to work out on more costly stuff, but I never imag-
ined the design to be the thing itself. This prayer of Christ is a
great chart, as it were, but I cannot cross the sea on a chart. It
is a map, but a man is not a traveler because he puts his fingers across the map. And so a man may use this form of prayer,
and yet be a total stranger to the great design of Christ in teaching it to His disciples. I feel that I cannot use this prayer to the
omission of others. Great as it is, it does not express all I desire to say to my Father who is in heaven.

There are many sins that I must confess separately and distinctly. The various other petitions that this prayer contains require, I feel, to be expanded, when I come before God in private.
I must pour out my heart in the language that His Spirit gives
me. More than that, I must trust in the Spirit to speak the unut-
terable groanings of my spirit when my lips cannot actually express all the emotions of my heart. Let none despise this prayer.
It is matchless. If we must have forms of prayer, let us have this
first, foremost, and chief, but let none think that Christ would
tie His disciples to the constant and only use of this. Let us rather
draw near to the throne of the heavenly grace with boldness as
children coming to a father, and let us tell forth our wants and
our sorrows in the language that the Holy Spirit teaches us.

And now, coming to the text, there are several things we shall have to notice here. And first, I shall dwell for a few minutes upon *the double relationship mentioned:* "Our Father which art in heaven." There is *sonship*—"Father"; there is *brotherhood*, for it says, "*Our* Father." If He be the common Father of us, then we must be brothers and sisters, for there are two relationships, sonship and brotherhood. In the next place, I shall utter a few words upon the spirit which is necessary to help us before we are able to utter this—"*The spirit of adoption*," whereby we can cry, "Our Father which art in heaven." And then, thirdly, I shall conclude with *the double argument of the text*, for it is really an argument upon which the rest of the prayer is based. "Our Father which art in heaven" is, as it were, a strong argument used before supplication itself is presented.

The Double Relationship Implied in the Text

We take the first one. Here is *sonship:* Our Father which art in heaven." How are we to understand this, and in what sense are we the sons and daughters of God? Some say that the Fatherhood of God is universal and that every man, from the fact of his being created by God, is necessarily God's son. Therefore every man has a right to approach the throne of God and say, "Our Father which art in heaven." To that I must demur. I believe that in this prayer we are to come before God looking upon Him not as our Father through creation, but as our Father through adoption and the new birth. I will very briefly state my reasons for this.

I have never been able to see that creation necessarily implies fatherhood. I believe God has made many things that are not His children. Has He not made the heavens and the earth, the sea and the fullness thereof? And are they His children? You say these are not rational and intelligent beings. But He made the angels, who stand in an eminently high and holy position. Are they His children? "Unto which of the angels said he at any time, Thou art my Son?" (Heb. 1:5). I do not find, as a rule, that angels are called the children of God. I must demur to the idea that mere creation brings God necessarily into the relationship of a father. Does not the potter make vessels of clay? But is the potter the father of the vase or of the bottle? No, beloved, it needs something beyond creation to constitute the relationship. Those who can say, "Our Father which art in heaven," are something more than God's creatures. They have been adopted into His family. He has taken them out of the old family in which they were born. He has washed them, cleansed them, and given them a new name and a new spirit. He has made them "heirs of God, and joint-heirs with Christ." He did all this of His own free, sovereign, unmerited, distinguishing grace.

And having adopted them to be His children, He has in the next place *regenerated them by the Spirit of the living God.* He has "begotten us again unto a lively hope by the resurrection of Jesus Christ from the dead" (1 Peter 1:3). No man has a right to claim God as His Father unless he feels in his soul and believes, solemnly, through the faith of God's election that He has been adopted into the one family of God that is in heaven and earth, and that he has been regenerated or born again.

This relationship also involves *love.* If God be my Father, He loves me. And oh, how He loves me! When God is a Husband, He is the best of husbands. Widows, somehow or other, are always well cared for. When God is a Friend, He is the best of friends and sticks closer than a brother. When He is a Father, He is the best of fathers. O fathers! perhaps you do not know how much you love your children. When they are sick you find it out, for you stand by their couches and you pity them as their little frames are writhing in pain. Well, "like as a father pitieth his children, so the LORD pitieth them that fear him." (Ps. 103:13). You know how you love your children, too, when they grieve you by their sin. Anger arises and you are ready to chasten them, but no sooner is the tear in their eye, than your hand is heavy and you feel that you had rather smite yourself than smite them. Every time you smite them you seem to cry, "Oh that I should have thus to afflict my child for his sin! Oh that I could suffer in his stead!" And God, even our Father, "doth not afflict willingly" (Lam. 3:33). Is not that a sweet thing? He is, as it were, compelled to it. Even the Eternal arm is not willing to do it. It is only His great love and deep wisdom that brings down the blow. But if you want to know your love to your children, you will know it most if they die. David knew that he loved his son Absalom, but he never knew how much he loved him until he heard that he had been slain, and that he had been buried by Joab. "Precious in the sight of the LORD is the deaths of his saints" (Ps. 116:15). He knows then how deep and pure is the love that death can never sever, and the terrors of eternity never can unbind. But, parents, although you love your children much, and you know it, you do not know and cannot tell how deep is the unfathomable abyss of the love of God to you. Go out at midnight and consider the heavens, the work of God's fingers, the moon and the stars which He has ordained. I am sure you will say, "What is man, that thou art mindful of him?" (Ps. 8:4; Heb. 2:6). But, more than all, you will wonder, not at your loving Him, but that while He has all these treasures, He should set His heart upon so insignificant a creature as man. And the sonship that God has given us is not a mere name. There is all our Father's great heart given to us in the moment when He claims us as His children.

But if this sonship involves the love of God to us, it involves also, the duty of *love to God.* Oh! heir of heaven, if you are God's child, will you not love your Father? What son is there that loves not his father? Is he not less than human if he loves not his father? Let his name be blotted from the book of remembrance that loves not the woman that brought him forth and the father that beget him. And we, the chosen favorites of heaven, adopted and regenerated, shall not we love Him? Shall we not say, "Whom have I in heaven but You, and is there none upon earth that I desire in comparison with You? My father, I will give You my heart. You shall be the guide of my youth. You do love me, and the little heart that I have shall be all Your own forever."

Furthermore, if we say "Our Father which art in heaven," we must recollect that our being sons and daughters involves the duty of *obedience* to God. When I say "My Father," it is not for me to rise up and go in rebellion against His wishes. If He be a father, let me note His commands and let me reverentially obey. If He has said, "Do this," let me do it, not because I dread Him but because I love him. If He forbids me to do anything, let me avoid it. There are some persons in the world who have not the spirit of adoption, and they can never be brought to do a thing unless they see some advantage to themselves in it. But with the child of God, there is no motive at all. He can boldly say, "I have never done a right thing since I have followed Christ because I hoped to get to heaven by it, nor have I ever avoided a wrong thing because I was afraid of being damned." For the child of God knows his good works do not make him acceptable to God, for he was acceptable to God by Jesus Christ long before he had any good works. The fear of hell does not affect him either, for he knows that he is delivered from that and shall never come into condemnation, having passed from death to life. He acts from pure love and gratitude, and until we come to that state of mind, I do not think there is such a thing as virtue. If a man has done what is called a virtuous action because he hoped to get to heaven or to avoid hell by it, whom has he served? Has he not served himself? And what is that but selfishness? But the man who has no hell to fear and no heaven to gain because heaven is his own and hell he never can enter, that man is capable of virtue, for he says—

> Now for the love I hear his name,
> What was my gain I count my loss;
> I pour contempt on all my shame,
> And nail my glory to his cross—

to His cross who loved and lived and died for me who loved Him not, but who desires now to love Him with all my heart and soul and strength.

And now permit me to draw your attention to one encouraging thought that may help to cheer the downcast and Satan-tempted child of God. *Sonship is a thing which all the infirmities of our flesh and all the sins into which we are hurried by temptation can never violate or weaken.* A man has a child. That child all of a sudden is bereaved of his senses. What a grief that is to a father. But the child is still a child. If we are the fathers of such children, they are ours. All that can possibly befall them can never shake the fact that they are our children. Oh! what a mercy when we transfer this to God's case and ours! How foolish we are sometimes—how worse than foolish. We may say as David did, "I was as a beast before thee" (Ps. 73:22). God brings before us the truths of His kingdom. We cannot see their beauty. We cannot appreciate them. We seem to be as if we were totally demented, ignorant, unstable, weary, and apt to slide. But, thanks be to God, we are His children still. And if there be anything worse that can happen to a father than his child becoming bereaved of his sense, it is when he grows up to be wicked. It is well said, "Children are doubtful blessings." I remember to have heard one say, and, as I thought, not very kindly, to a mother with an infant at her breast: "Woman! you may be suckling a viper there." It stung the mother to the quick, and it was not needful to have said it. But how often is it the fact that the child that has hung upon its mother's breast when it grows up brings that mother's gray hairs with sorrow to the grave!

> Oh! sharper than a serpent's tooth
> To have a thankless child!

Oh, to have a child that is ungodly, vile, debauched—a blasphemer! But mark, beloved, if he be a child he cannot lose his childship, nor we our fatherhood, be he who or what he may. Let him be transported beyond the seas, he is still our son. Let us deny him the house because his conversation might lead others of our children into sin, yet our son he is and must be. When sod shall cover his head and ours, "father and son" shall still be on the tombstone. The relationship never can be severed as long as time shall last. The prodigal was his father's son when he was among the harlots and when he was feeding swine. God's children are God's children anywhere and everywhere, and shall be even unto the end. Nothing can sever that sacred tie or divide us from his heart.

There is yet another thought that may cheer the Little-faiths and Feeble-minds. *The fatherhood of God is common to all His children.* Ah! Little-faith, you have often looked up to Mr. Great-heart, and you have said, "Oh that I had the courage of Great-heart, that I could wield his sword and cut old giant Grim in pieces! Oh that I could fight the dragons and that I could overcome the lions! But I am stumbling at every straw and a shadow makes me afraid." Listen, Little-faith, Great-heart is God's child, and you are God's child, too. Great-heart is not a whit more God's child than you are. David was the son of God, but not more the son of God than you. Peter and Paul, the highly-favored apostles, were of the family of the Most High, and so are you. You have children yourselves. One is a son grown up and out in business, perhaps, and you have another, a little thing still in your arms. Which is most your child, the little one or the big one? "Both alike," you say. "This little one is my child, near my heart. And the big one is my child, too." And so the little Christian is as much a child of God as the great one.

> This cov'nant stands secure,
>   Though earth's old pillars bow;
> The strong, the feeble, and the weak,
>   Are one in Jesus now.

They are one in the family of God, and no one is ahead of the other. One may have more grace than another, but God does not love one more than another. One may be an older child than another, but he is not more a child. One may do more mighty works and may bring more glory to his Father, but he whose name is the least in the kingdom of heaven is as much the child of God as he who stands among the king's mighty men. Let this cheer and comfort us when we draw near to God and say, "Our Father which art in heaven."

I will make but one more remark before I leave this point. Namely this, that *our being the children of God brings with it innumerable privileges.* Time would fail me if I were to attempt to read the long roll of the Christian's joyous privileges. I am God's child. If so, He will clothe me. My shoes shall be iron and brass. He will array me with the robe of my Savior's righteousness, for He has said, "Bring forth the best robe and put it on him." He has also said that He will put a crown of pure gold upon my head, and inasmuch as I am a King's son, I shall have a royal crown. Am I His child? Then He will feed me. My bread shall be given me, and my water shall be sure. He that feeds the ravens will never let His children starve. If a good husbandman feeds the barn-door fowl, the sheep, and the bullocks, certainly his children shall not starve. Does my Father deck the lily, and shall I go naked? Does He feed the fowls of the heaven that sow not, neither do they reap? Shall I feel necessity? God forbid! My Father knows what things I have need of before I ask Him, and He will give me all I want. If I be His child, then I have a portion in His heart here, and I shall have a portion in His house above. "If children then heirs; heirs of God and joint-heirs with Christ; if so be that we suffer with him, that we may be also glorified together" (Rom. 8:17). And oh! what a prospect this opens up! The fact of our being heirs of God and joint-heirs with Christ proves that all things are ours—the gift of God, the purchase of a Savior's blood.

> This world is ours, and worlds to come;
> Earth is our lodge, and heaven our home.

Are there crowns? They are mine if I be an heir. Are there thrones? Are there dominions? Are there harps, palm branches, white robes? Are there glories that eye has not seen? Is there music that the ear has not heard? All these are mine, if I be a child of God. "And it doth not yet appear what we shall be: but we know that, when he shall appear, we shall be like him; for we shall see him as he is" (1 John 3:2). Talk of princes and kings and potentates. Their inheritance is but a pitiful foot of land, across which the bird's wing can soon direct its flight. But the broad acres of the Christian cannot be measured by eternity. He is rich, without a limit to his wealth. He is blessed, without a boundary to his bliss. All this, and more than I can enumerate, is involved in our being able to say, "Our Father which art in heaven."

The second tie of the text is *brotherhood*. It does not say *my* Father, but *our* Father. Then it seems there are a great many in the family. I will be very brief on this point.

"Our Father." When you pray that prayer, remember you have a good many brothers and sisters that do not know their Father yet, and you must include them all. For all God's elect ones, though they be uncalled as yet, are still His children, though they know it not. In one of Krummacher's beautiful little parables there is a story like this:

> Abraham sat one day in the grove at Mamre, leaning his head on his hand, and sorrowing. Then his son Isaac came to him, and said, "My father, why mournest thou? what aileth thee?" Abraham answered and said, "My soul mourneth for the people of Canaan, that they know not the Lord, but walk in their own ways, in darkness and foolishness." "Oh, my father," answered the son, "is it only this? Let not thy heart be sorrowful; for are not these their own ways?" Then the patriarch rose up from his seat, and said, "Come now, follow me." And he led the youth to a hut, and said to him, "Behold." There was a child which was imbecile, and the mother sat weeping by it. Abraham asked her, "Why weepest thou? Then the mother said, "Alas, this my son eateth and drinketh, and we minister unto him; but he knows not the face of his father, nor of his mother. Thus his life is lost, and this source of joy is sealed to him."

Is not that a sweet little parable to teach us how we ought to pray for the many sheep that are not yet in the fold but which must be brought in? We ought to pray for them because they do not know their Father. Christ has bought them and they do not know Christ. The Father has loved them from before the foundation of the world, and yet they know not the face of their Father. When you say, "Our Father," think of the many of your brothers and sisters that are in the back streets of London, that are in the dens and caves of Satan. Think of your poor brother that is intoxicated with the spirit of the devil. Think of him, led astray to infamy, lust, and, perhaps, to murder, and in your prayer pray for them who know not the Lord.

"Our Father." That, then, includes those of God's children who differ from us in their doctrine. Ah! there are some that differ from us as wide as the poles, but yet they are God's children. Come, Mr. Bigot, do not kneel down and say, "My Father," but "Our Father." "If you please, I cannot put in Mr. So-and-So, for I think he is a heretic." Put him in, sir. God has put him in, and you must put him in, too, and say, "Our Father." Is it not remarkable how very much alike all God's people are upon their knees? Some time ago at a prayer meeting I called upon two brothers in Christ to pray one after another, the one a Wesleyan and the other a strong Calvinist. The Wesleyan prayed the most Calvinistic prayer of the two, I do believe—at least, I could not tell which was which. I listened to see if I could not discern some peculiarity even in their phraseology, but there was none. "Saints in prayer appear as one." For when they get on their knees, they are all compelled to say, "Our Father," and all their language afterward is of the same sort.

When you pray to God, put in the poor, for is He not the Father of many of the poor, rich in faith, and heirs of the kingdom though they be poor in this world. Come, my sister, if you bow your knee amid the rustling of silk and satin, yet remember the cotton and the print. My brother, is there wealth in your hand, yet I pray, remember your brethren of the hard hand and the dusty brow. Remember those who could not wear what you wear, nor eat what you eat, but are as Lazarus compared with you while you are as Dives. Pray for them. Put them all in the same prayer and say, "Our Father."

And pray for those that are divided from us by time sea—those that are in heathen hands, scattered like precious salt in the midst of this world's putrefaction. Pray for all that name the name of Jesus, and let your prayer be a great and comprehensive one. "Our Father, which art in heavens." And after you have prayed that, rise up and act it. Say not "Our Father," and then look upon your brethren with a sneer or a frown. I beseech you, live like a brother and act like a brother. Help the needy, cheer the sick, comfort the fainthearted. Go about doing good and minister to the suffering people of God wherever you find them. Let the world take knowledge of you, that you are when on your feet what you are upon your knees—that you are a brother to all the brotherhood of Christ, a brother born for adversity, like your Master Himself.

The Spirit of Adoption

I am extremely puzzled and bewildered how to explain to the ungodly what is the spirit with which we must be filled before we can pray this prayer. If I had a foundling here, one who had never seen either father or mother, I think I should have a very great difficulty in trying to make him understand what are the feelings of a child toward its father. Poor little thing, he has been under tutors and governors. He has learned to respect them for their kindness or to fear them for their austerity. But there never can be in that child's heart that love toward tutor or governor, however kind he may be, that there is in the heart of another child toward his own mother or father. There is a nameless charm there. We cannot describe or understand it. It is a sacred touch of nature, a throb in the breast that God has put there, and that cannot be taken away. The fatherhood is recognized by the childship of the child. And what is that spirit of a child—that sweet spirit that makes him recognize and love his father? I cannot tell you unless you are a child your-self, and then you will know.

And what is "the spirit of adoption, whereby we cry Abba, Father?" I cannot tell you. But if you have felt it, you will know it. It is a sweet compound of faith that knows God to be my Father, love that loves Him as my Father, joy that rejoices in Him as my Father, fear that trembles to disobey Him because He is my Father, and a confident affection and trustfulness that relies upon Him and casts itself wholly upon Him because it knows by the infallible witness of the Holy Spirit that Jehovah, the God of earth and heaven, is the Father of my heart. Oh! have you ever felt the spirit of adoption? There is nothing like it beneath the sky. Save heaven itself there is nothing more blissful than to enjoy that spirit of adoption. Oh! when the wind of trouble is blowing and waves of adversity are rising, and the ship is reeling to the rock, how sweet then to say, "My Father," and to believe that His strong hand is on the helm! When the bones are aching and the loins are filled with pain, and when the cup is brimming with wormwood and gall, to say, "My Father," and seeing that Father's hand holding the cup to the lip to drink it steadily to the very dregs because we can say, "Father . . . not my will, but thine, be done" (Luke 22:42). Well says Martin Luther, in his *Exposition of the Galatians,* "There is more eloquence in that word, 'Abba, Father,' than in all the orations of Demosthenes or Cicero put together." "My Father!" Oh! there is music there. There is elo-quence there. There is the very essence of heaven's own bliss in that word, "My Father," when applied to God, and when said by us with an unfaltering tongue through the inspiration of the Spirit of the living God.

My hearers, have you the spirit of adoption? If not, you are miserable men. May God Himself bring you to know Him! May He teach you your need of Him. May He lead you to the cross of Christ and help you to look to your dying Brother! May He bathe you in the blood that flowed from His open wounds, and then, accepted in the beloved, may you rejoice that you have the honor to be one of that sacred family.

A Double Argument

And now, in the last place, I said that there was in the title a double argument. "Our Father." That is, "Lord, hear what I have to say. You are my Father." If I come before a judge I have no right to expect that he shall hear me at any particular season in anything that I have to say. If I came merely to crave for some boon or benefit to myself, if the law were on my side, then I could demand an audience at his hands. But when I come as a lawbreaker, and only come to crave for mercy or for favors I deserve not, I have no right to expect to be heard. But a child, even though he is erring, always expects his father will hear what he has to say. "Lord, if I call You King You will say, 'You are a rebellious subject; get gone.' If I call You Judge You will say, 'Be still, or out of your own mouth will I condemn you.' If I call You Creator You will say to me, 'It repents Me that I made man upon the earth.' If I call You my Preserver You will say to me, 'I have preserved you, but you have rebelled against Me.' But if I call You Father, all my sinfulness doth not invalidate my claim. If You be my Father, then You love me. If I be Your child, then You will regard me, and poor though my language be, You will not despise it."

If a child were called upon to speak in the presence of a number of persons, how very much alarmed he would be lest he should not use right language. I may sometimes feel when I have to address a mighty auditory, lest I should not select choice words, full well knowing that if I were to preach as I never shall, like the mightiest of orators, I would always have enough of carping critics to rail at me. But if I had my father here, and if you could all stand in the relationship of father to me, I would not be very particular what language I used. When I talk to my Father I am not afraid he will misunderstand me. If I put my words a little out of place he understands my meaning somehow. When we are little children we only prattle. Still our father understands us. Our children talk a great deal more like Dutchmen than Englishmen when they begin to talk. Strangers come in and say, "Dear me, what is the child talking about?"

But we know what it is. Though in what they say there may not be an intelligible sound that anyone could print and a reader make it out, we know they have certain little wants. Having a way of expressing their desires, we can understand them. So when we come to God, our prayers are little broken things. We cannot put them together. But our Father, He will hear us. Oh! what a beginning is "Our Father" to a prayer full of faults—foolish prayer, perhaps, a prayer in which we are going to ask what we ought not to ask for! "Father, forgive the language! Forgive the matter!" As one dear brother said the other day at the prayer meeting. He could not get on in prayer, and he finished up on a sudden by saying, "Lord, I cannot pray tonight as I should wish. I cannot put the words together. Lord, take the meaning, take the meaning," and sat down. That is just what David said once, "Lord, all my desire is before thee" (Ps. 38:9)—not my words, but my desire, and God could read it. We should say, "Our Father," because that is a reason why God should hear what we have to say.

But there is another argument. "Our Father." "Lord, give me what I want." If I come to a stranger, I have no right to expect he will give it me. He may out of his charity. But if I come to a father, I have a claim, a sacred claim. My Father, I shall have no need to use arguments to move Your bosom. I shall not have to speak to You as the beggar who cries in the street, for because You are my Father You know my wants, and You are willing to relieve me. It is Your business to relieve me. I can come confidently to You, knowing You will give me all I want. If we ask our Father for anything when we are little children, we are under an obligation certainly, but it is an obligation we never feel. If you were hungry and your father fed you, would you feel an obligation like you would if you went into the house of a stranger? You go into a stranger's house trembling, and you tell him you are hungry. Will he feed you? He says yes, he will give you somewhat. But if you go to your father's table, almost without asking, you sit down as a matter of course and feast to your full, and you rise and go, and feel you are indebted to him. But there is not a grievous sense of obligation. Now, we are all deeply under obligation to God, but it is a child's obligation—an obligation that impels us to gratitude, but that does not constrain us to feel that we have been demeaned by it. Oh! if He were not my Father, how could I expect that He would relieve my wants? But since He is my Father, He will, He must hear my prayers and answer the voice of my crying and supply all my needs out of the riches of His fullness in Christ Jesus the Lord.

Has your father treated you badly lately? I have this word for you, then. Your father loves you quite as much when he treats you roughly as when he treats you kindly. There is often more love in an angry father's heart than there is in the heart of a father who is too kind. I will suppose a case. Suppose there were two fathers, and their two sons went away to some re-mote part of the earth where idolatry is still practiced. Sup-pose these two sons were decoyed and deluded into idolatry. The news comes to England, and the first father is very angry. His son, his own son, has forsaken the religion of Christ and become an idolater. The second father says, "Well, if it will help him in trade, I don't care. If he gets on the better by it, all well and good." Now, which loves most, the angry father or the fa-ther who treats the matter with complacency? Why, the angry father is the best. He loves his son; therefore, he cannot give away his son's soul for gold. Give me a father that is angry with my sins and that seeks to bring me back, even though it be by chastisement. Thank God you have a father that can be angry, but that loves you as much when He is angry as when He smiles upon you.

Go away with that upon your mind and rejoice. But if you love not God and fear Him not, go home, I beseech you, to confess your sins and to seek mercy through the blood of Christ. May this sermon be made useful in bringing you into the fam-ily of Christ, though you have strayed from him long. Though His love has followed you long in vain, may it now find you and bring you to His house rejoicing!

NOTES

Bringing Heaven to Earth

John Henry Jowett (1864–1923) was known as "the greatest preacher in the English-speaking world." He was born in Yorkshire, England. He was ordained into the Congregational ministry, and his second pastorate was at the famous Carr's Lane Church, Birmingham, where he followed the eminent Dr. Robert W. Dale. From 1911 to 1918, he pastored the Fifth Avenue Presbyterian Church, New York City; from 1918 to 1923, he ministered at Westminster Chapel, London, succeeding G. Campbell Morgan. He wrote many books of devotional messages and sermons.

This message was taken from *God Our Contemporary*, published by the Fleming H. Revell Company in 1922.

6

Bringing Heaven to Earth

Thy will be done, on earth as it is in heaven. (Matthew 6:10 RSV)

I SUPPOSE THAT to the majority of people these familiar words suggest a funeral rather than a wedding. They recall experiences to which we were compelled to submit but in which we found no delight. They awaken memories of gathering clouds, gloomy days, blocked roads, failing strength, and open graves. "Thy will be done!" They remind us of afflictions in the presence of which we were numb and dumb. And so we have a sort of negative and passive attitude toward the words. We have a feeling toward them as to some visitor we have to *put up with,* rather than to a welcome friend whose coming fills the house with life and happy movement. They suggest the cypress and the yew tree, things sullen and gloomy, rather than the coronal attributes of the cedar and the palm.

And so it is that the graces and virtues that are most frequently associated with these words are of the dull and passive order. The grace of resignation is the plant that is most prolific in this bitter soil. Even many of the hymns that sing about the will of God are in the minor tone, and they dwell upon the gloomier aspects of providence which call for the grace of resignation. I am not unmindful of the fields of sadness that often stretch around our homes like marshy fens. Our circumstances gather about us in stormy cloud and tempest. The rains fall and the floods cover our lot in dreary desolation. And we may reverently recall one black night in the days of the Son of Man when in Gethsemane the rains descended, the floods came, the winds blew, and the afflicted heart of the Savior submitted itself in strong resignation, crying, "Nevertheless not my will, but thine, be done" (Luke 22:42).

And yet if resignation be our only attitude to the will of God, our life will be sorely wanting in delightful strength and beauty. A cypress here and there is all very well, but not a woodland of them! A yew tree here and there is all very well, but not a whole forest of them! In one of his letters, Robert Louis Stevenson has a paragraph that represents an imaginary conversation with his gardener about the black winter green known as Resignation.

> "John, do you see that bed of Resignation?"
>
> "It's doing bravely, sir."
>
> "John, I will not have it in my garden; it flatters not the eye, and it is no comfort; root it out."
>
> "Sir, I ha'e seen o' them that rose as high as nettles; gran' plants."
>
> "What then? Were they as tall as Alps, if still unsavoury and bleak, what matters it? Out with it, then; and in its place put a bush of Flowering Piety—but see it be the flowering sort—the other species is no ornament to any gentleman's back garden."

But then how are we going to get more of the flowering piety into our gardens? I think this is the answer. We shall get it by cultivating a more active and positive attitude toward the will of God. The will of God is not always something burdensome which we have to bear. It is something glorious that we have to do. And therefore we are not to stand before it as mourners only, humbly making our submission, but as keen and eager knights gladly receiving our commissions. The will of God is not always associated with deprivation. It is more commonly associated with a trust. It is not something withheld, it is something given. There is an active savor about it. There is a ringing challenge in it. It is a call to chivalry and crusade. And therefore the symbol of our relation to the will of God is not that of the bowed head, but that of the lit lamp and the girt loin, as of happy servants delighted with their tasks. It is in this positive relationship to the will of God that the will becomes our song, the song of ardent knights upon the road riding abroad to express the will of their King in all the common dealings and relationships of men. "Thy will be done on earth!" That is not merely the poignant cry of mourners surrendering their treasures. It is the cry of a jubilant host with a King in their midst consecrating the strength of their arms to the cause of His kingdom. The will of God is here not something to be endured, but something to be done.

How, then, are we to take our share in this commission? How are we to do the will of God on earth as it is done in heaven? *First of all, by finding out what life is like in heaven.* "As it is done in heaven!" If our privileged commission is to make earth more like heaven it must surely be our first inquiry to find out what heaven is like. Well, what is heaven like? I will very frankly confess to you that I am in no wise helped to answer our question by the so-called spiritualistic revelations of these latter days. These strange seances with the lights out, a trumpet on the table, and the rowdy singing, they bring me no authoritative word or vision. The character of the heavenly life that is revealed is so unsatisfying—the glare of it, the garishness of it, its furnishings as of a cheap and tawdry theater, the utter weakness and insipidity of its utterance. They tell me nothing that I want to know. Its leaders assure me that their revelations are chasing away uncertainties. They are transforming lean hypotheses into firm experiences. They are proving the reality of the life beyond and are making immortality sure. I am waiting for a revelation of something which deserves to be immortal. I am reverently listening for some word which is both spirit and life.

I am listening for something worthy of kinship with the word of the apostle Paul. No, worthy of the risen Lord. What is offered to me is like cheap jewelry in contrast with precious stones and fine gold. Eternal life is to me not merely endless length of line. It is quality of line. It is height and depth and breadth. "This is life eternal, that they might know thee . . . and Jesus Christ, whom thou hast sent" (John 17:3).

I therefore turn away from the so-called modern revelations if I wish to know what life is like in heaven. What is life like as it is lived in the immediate presence and fellowship of God? What are the habits of the heavenly community? What is the manner of their affections? What is the nature of their discernments? What are their standards of values? What are their ways of looking at things? What are their quests, their labors, and their delights? What are their relationships one to another? Is there any answer to these questions? If I wish to learn what life is like in heaven, I turn to Him who came from heaven. He made certain tremendous claims, and the very greatness of them arrests my soul and fills me with receptive awe. Let us listen to Him:

> No man hath ascended up to heaven, but he that came down from heaven. (John 3:13)

> He that cometh from above is above all: . . . what he hath seen and heard, that he testifieth. (vv. 31–32)

> The bread of God is he which cometh down from heaven and giveth life unto the world. (6:33)

> I came down from heaven, not to do mine own will, but the will of him that sent me. (v. 38)

What is that last most wonderful word? It seems to come very near to the way of my quest. I am eagerly inquiring how God's will is done in heaven, and here is One who claims that He comes down from heaven to do the will of Him that sent

Him. He brings heaven with Him. His speech is full of it. He talks about "Your Father in heaven." He talks about "the treasures in heaven" and about "the kingdom of heaven." He uses simile after simile, and parable after parable, to tell us what it is like. "The kingdom of heaven is like unto . . . is like unto . . . is like unto. . . ." The familiar words run like some lovely and inspiring refrain. If I would know what heaven is like, I must listen to His Word.

But the revelation in Christ Jesus is more than a revelation in words. The Word became flesh. It was not only something we could hear; it was something we could see. He not only startled men's ears, as with a music that had never before been heard in their gray, unlovely streets; He startled men's eyes as with a light that had never before fallen on sea or land. He not only talked about the heavenly life, He lived it. His life on earth was just a transcript of the life in heaven. As we reverently gaze upon Him, we can watch the process of the incarnation. The heavenly is imaged forth in the earthly, and it is taking form in human life and story. Every movement of Jesus spells a word of the heavenly literature. Every feature in Jesus is a lineament of the invisible life. Every gesture tells a story. Every one of His earthly relationships unfolds the nature of the heavenly communion. His habits unveil their habits, and His quests reveal their quests. The Eternal breaks through every moment, and the light is tempered to our mortal gaze. The revelation never ceases. It begins in Nazareth and continues to Calvary, and beyond Calvary to Olivet. You can never catch our Lord in some moment when the divine afflatus has been withdrawn, when the inspiration ends, and when His life drops down to dull and unsuggestive commonplace. Everything in Jesus is a ministry of revelation. He *is* revelation. "I am . . . the truth" (John 14:6). His earthly life reveals the landscape of the heavenly fields. If, therefore, I would know what heaven is like, I must listen to the word of Jesus, and with eager, reverent eyes I must follow the Word made flesh.

But let me give this counsel about the quest. When we set

about studying the words of Jesus do not let us become en-
tangled in the letter. It is possible to be imprisoned in the words
and so to miss the hidden treasure. We are in search of the
spirit of the kingdom of heaven. We want to know its attitudes,
its royal moods, its splendid manners, its principles, its life. We
must not, therefore, be deterred and interred in the literalism
of the letter. We must seek the hidden treasure in the earthen
vessel. We must seek the heavenly wine in the earthly wine skins.
We must seek the beating heart of a simile, the secret vitality
of a parable, the holy fire that burns on the innermost altar of
the Word. We are in search of heavenly principles, principles
that we can apply to the humdrum life of earth and so trans-
form it into heaven.

Go, then, in search of the principles of the heavenly life. And
whenever you find a heavenly principle, something which controls and orders the life of heaven, write it down in your own
words and regard it as one of the controlling guides of humdrum life. Do the same with the Master's life. What a brief little
record it is! I turn away my eyes to my study shelves and I see
the life of Lincoln in five large volumes. I then turn to the bi-
ography of Jesus, and in the Bible that I am using it covers 107
pages. In those 107 pages the story is told four times over! How
marvelously brief it is, and yet how marvelously meaningful and
full! Go over it with the utmost slowness. You are in search of
something more precious than gold, yes, than much fine gold.
If our Savior moves, if He turns His face toward anybody, if
He looks at a little child, or at someone who is near the kingdom of heaven, follow the movement and watch Him, and
challenge your judgment as to its significance. Is the movement
a revelation? Is it an earthly segment suggesting a heavenly
circle, and can you venture to reverently complete the circle?
Thus must we go in search of the heavenly principles. Again,
when we have found one, let us express it in our own words
and write it down as one of the fundamental controls of human life.

And when you have your heavenly principles, when you

have analyzed them and have arranged them in some order, will you have many of them? I think not. Will your notebook be overflowing with entries? I think not. You will probably have just a little handful, perhaps not more than a dozen of them, perhaps only half-a-dozen. But they will be something you can handle, for not only are they the principles of heaven, they are the laws of heaven for our life on earth. They are the fundamental things in the ministry of transformation, and they are to make earth and heaven one. If, therefore, you would know what life in heaven is like, study Him who came from heaven, even the Son of Man who is in heaven.

Well, now, having found out what life is like in heaven, we must now find out what life is like on earth. What are the facts about things on this planet of ours in which we pitch our moving tents for threescore years and ten? If we are to bring the principles of the heavenly life to mold and fashion our life upon earth, we must know what we are about. Is our life on earth in any way like the life in heaven that is revealed in Jesus Christ, or is it very unlike it? We must go in search of the facts. What are the facts? And there you face the difficulty which only an unwearying perseverance can conquer. For, strangely enough, it is far more easy to discover the facts about the life in heaven than to discover the facts about the life on earth. Heaven yearns to reveal itself, to make itself known, to share its secrets, and it has done these things in Jesus Christ. But earth seeks to hide its facts, to obscure them, to skillfully camouflage them, until it is almost impossible to discover the simplicity of truth in all this elaborate paraphernalia of falsehood and disguise.

How intensely difficult it is to see a thing just as it is, in all the clear, vivid, untampered outlines of sheer veracity! Our newspapers do not really help us in the quest. Their vision is perverted in many ways. It is perverted by political partisanship, by the spirit of class, by the narrowing mood of sect, by the proud domination of wealth, by the desire to please more than to inform. How hard it is to find the facts through the daily press! I take two morning papers, and I have chosen them on the ground of their being as absolutely unlike each other as can be well conceived. I look out upon the world through their two lenses in the fond hope that one may regulate the other, and that in their mutual correction I may arrive at something like the truth. But through what a riot of confusion one has to fight his way if he is to find the fact of things in their simple and transparent order! For instance, the facts about the miners and the owners of the mines! The facts about Prohibition in the United States! The facts about the drinking customs of our people! Where are our working people assembling in vast multitudes to demonstrate their determination to have more drink? Where are the masses of people who are assembling to demand a brighter London, and who are going to secure it by extending the drinking facilities for an hour or two longer at night? What are the facts about things? The facts about the starving populations of Russia! The facts about India, about the inner currents of its thought and feeling, the secret aspirations of its countless multitudes, the sleepless activities of Islam! What a hunt it is, this hunting for facts! And yet, if the heavenly principles are to be brought to earth, to govern and regulate her life, if the crooked is to be made straight and the rough places plain, we must know where the dangerous crookedness is to be found on the road and where the road is so rough that it breaks the feet of pilgrims and lames them for their honest and necessary journey.

I can well imagine that if the church of Christ—the whole church of Christ—were united in life and purpose, if she were really what we sometimes sing she is—a mighty army, not shuffling along any and every road in loose and bedraggled array, but marching under one plan of campaign and moving in invincible strength—I can imagine she would have her own Intelligence Department, her own secret service, her own exploring eyes and ears, peering everywhere, listening everywhere, knowing the most hidden facts of the nation's life and proclaiming them from ten thousand pulpits in every part of the land. But while we wait for the united church of Christ we must not go to sleep. Young people must strenuously and untiringly seek to get at the facts. How is it with old mother-earth? Is she full of the glory of God? Or is she full of shameful things, crooked things, wasteful things, wicked things? Is her life really vital, or is it superficial, artificial, a poor withered, wrinkled thing hidden in powders and cosmetics? What are the facts? Knowing what life is like in heaven find out what life is like on earth. Get at the facts.

And now for a last thing. Having a firm grip of divine principles—"as it is in heaven"—and with a clear knowledge of earthly facts—"as it is done on earth"—then with fearless application bring your principles close to your facts, and make your facts bow to your principles, reshaping them by the heavenly standards so that the crooked becomes straight and the rough places plain. Bring the heavenly close to the earthly and change every earthly thing into heavenly currency, stamping it with the divine image and superscription. "Thy will be done on earth as it is done in heaven!" That is gloriously positive work. It is challenging work. It is exhilarating work. It is work that is worthy of the knights of God. It is to bring heaven and earth together until the two become one. It is to bring the heavenly to the earthly, to bring divine principles into the region of economics, into the realm of business. It is to bring them into the thicket of politics, to the simplification of society and to the reconstruction of international relationships.

"It can't be done!" What is that? "It can't be done!" What can't be done? "You cannot mix the heavenly and the earthly. You cannot wed them into vital union. Religion is religion, and business is business, and never the twain shall meet. Religion is religion, and politics is politics, and to try to marry the two is to seek a covenant between oil and water. You cannot bring religion into commerce and let the heavenly visitor settle the height of the tariff wall or remove it altogether. No, religion is religion, and trade is trade! There was no chair for religion in the Council Chamber at Versailles. She was not expected. She was not really invited. And if, by any chance, she had appeared and spoken she would have been pathetically out of place." "But why would she have been out of place?" "Oh, well, everything in its place. And Versailles was the place for the stern soldier, the astute and wily diplomatist, the subtle politician. It was no place for the saint! You cannot have a coalition between Christ and Caesar. It can't be done!"

"Thy will be done on earth as it is done in heaven." Jesus Christ said it could be done, and that is the end of it. Nothing is excepted from the heavenly claim. God claims everything. There is no confusion at the heart of things. There is one Intelligence in the universe, one central Will, one great White Throne. God's decree runs through all things, and His holy will is best in everything. What is good religion can never be bad business. What is rotten religion can never be sound economics. What is morally right can never be politically wrong. "Thy will be done on earth!" That is the right road in everything. On that road alone can true life be found, the abiding secret of vital progress and happiness. Then let us firmly grasp the divine principles revealed to us in Christ. Let us fearlessly apply them to every sort of earthly facts. Let us mold the facts according to the pattern that we have found in the holy Mount.

But let us remember this. These words of our Master are first of all a prayer before they become a commandment. Our hands are to be uplifted in supplication before our feet begin their journey. We are to fall to our knees before we take to the road. It is first a prayer, then a crusade, and then a victory. "Thy will is done on earth as it is done in heaven."

NOTES

Thy Will Be Done

George W. Truett (1867–1944) was perhaps the best-known Southern Baptist preacher of his day. He pastored the First Baptist Church of Dallas, Texas, from 1897 until his death and saw it grow in both size and influence. Active in denominational ministry, Truett served as president of the Southern Baptist Convention and for five years was president of the Baptist World Alliance, but he was known primarily as a gifted preacher and evangelist. Nearly a dozen books of his sermons were published.

This sermon was taken from *Who Is Jesus,* published in 1952 by William B. Eerdmans and reprinted in 1973 by Baker Book House.

7

Thy Will Be Done

Thy will be done in earth, as it is in heaven. (Matthew 6:10)

LET US THINK TOGETHER for a little while on the most important prayer that we are called to pray here in our earthly life. This prayer is indicated for us in one terse sentence, spoken by Jesus in the incomparable prayer that He has given as a model for His people. We speak of this prayer often as "The Lord's Prayer." Perhaps it might more properly be called "The Model Prayer," "The Pattern Prayer," or "The Disciples' Prayer."

One day when Jesus was here in the flesh, He gave Himself to a season of prayer, and one who saw Him and heard Him was so moved that he made the request, "Lord, teach us to pray as John also taught his disciples." At that time, Jesus gave in abbreviated form the prayer that Matthew recorded in fuller form as part of the Sermon on the Mount. Who on earth knows how to pray this prayer like it ought to be prayed? We probably run over it in memory often times without much reverent thought at all.

> Our Father which art in heaven, Hallowed be thy name. Thy kingdom come. Thy will be done in earth, as it is in heaven. Give us this day our daily bread. And forgive us our debts,

as we forgive our debtors. And lead us not into temptation,
but deliver us from evil: For thine is the kingdom, and the
power, and the glory, forever. Amen. (Matthew 6:9–13)

Oh, who can scale the heights and sound the depths of that
model prayer? There is one sentence in the prayer that indicates the most important prayer for us to pray: "Thy will be
done in earth, as it is in heaven." The loftiest privilege of human life is to do the will of God. No other duty is so high as
that. No other privilege is so glorious as that—to do the will of
God. God has a will, and man also has a will. It is the will of
God to rule over us. All nature, except human nature, obeys
the will of God. There is one discordant voice to be heard in
the world and that voice is man's. He disobeys the will of God.
We know that evil is here by man's will, by man's choice. The
basic sin of all is selfishness. It was back of the sin of disobedience in the Garden of Eden. Evil is here by man's choice. We
can say "yes" or "no." Man said "no" in the beginning to God's
will, so evil is here by man's choice, by man's preference.

Now what is the meaning of this great prayer? "Thy will be
done in earth, as it is in heaven." The meaning in a sentence is
for us to pray that God may have His way with us here in this
world even as He does with the hosts who are in the heavenly
world.

This prayer for the doing of God's will comes before our
prayer for daily bread. Mark it again. "Our Father who art in
heaven, hallowed be thy name. Thy kingdom come. Thy will
be done in earth, as it is in heaven." Then comes our prayer
for daily bread. "Give us this day our daily bread." Note the
order! Does not that order terribly rebuke us? Are not many
of our prayers distressingly selfish? How often do we pray for
the will of God to be done on earth before we pray that we
may prosper in business, that we may be healed from sickness,
that we may be recovered in health? How often do we follow
this order? "Thy kingdom come, thy will, O Father, be done
here on earth as it is now done in heaven above." How often

do we pray that before we come down to our daily necessities—
to our problems of food and raiment, to our daily work and
burden, to our bearing and general welfare? Does not this order terribly rebuke us?

You ask, "Shall we not pray about our daily bread?" Yes,
certainly! "And shall we not pray as we go about our business?"
Yes, of course! The more you pray about it, the better it will
be for you and for your business, too. "Shall we not pray about
our health when it is undermined, about our bodies when they
are sick?" To be sure! Make it a matter of earnest prayer. Pray
about health. Pray about business. Pray about the daily adven-
ture, the daily work, the daily burden-bearing, but let it be in
the proper perspective. Let it come in its proper order. More
important than our daily bread is it for God's kingdom to come
on earth. More important than that we shall have food and
raiment in gracious measure is it that God's will be done here
on earth as it is done in heaven above. More important than
that our sick bodies shall be cured is it that God's kingdom
shall come and His will shall be translated into life in our city,
state, and world.

Therefore, we are to call ourselves back to this primary, tran-
scendent, supremely important prayer and let it come in the
order in which Jesus placed it for us. It may be God's will for
us to be sick for awhile. Very well, His will be done. It may be
His will for us to travel the dark, rough way of adversity for a
while instead of the way of prosperity. Very well, His will be
done. Hezekiah traveled the road of adversity and in talking
to the Lord about adversity said, "O, Lord, by these things men
live" (Isa. 38:16). Martin Luther testified that his greatest teachers of all were teachers of adversity. Oh, if out of the economic
depression and disquietude and unrest and disappointment and
broken plans, the people shall be nearer to God, God's will be
done!

What a challenge this prayer is to us! "Thy will be done." Whatever it is, wherever it leads, whatever it costs, whatever it means!
Your will be done. If it means a season of trial, of adversity, of

pain, of suffering, of fear—very well, Father, Your will be done.
If it means broken plans, blasted prospects, faded hopes, and
disappointed expectations, Your will be done. Oh, it is a challenge, the most difficult challenge that the soul ever faced. To
pray this prayer without evasion or reservation is a real test of
Christian character. Do you pray it? Have you prayed it today?
Can you pray it without any reservations? "Father, Your will be
done, with me and my family and all my programs and plans
and interests; Your will be done." Can you pray that prayer?

I confess frankly, in my early Christian life I held back from
praying this prayer. There never was a prayer in all the world
that so frightened me as this prayer. Never another prayer that
so terrorized my soul as this prayer: "Your will be done, whatever it is, for me and mine." If I know my heart now, if I understand my poor self, I would not dare pray any other prayer
that was contrary to the prayer which says, "Father, Your will
be done with me and mine, whether by life or death, Your will
be done!"

It will help us to remember two things as we try to pray this
prayer. First, whose will is it we want done? It is not the will of a
tyrant, not the will of an enemy. It is the will of the best friend
we have in the universe. It is the will of our heavenly Father—
the One who created us, the One who keeps us, the One who
crowns us with every mercy and grace and goodness. He is our
Father who sees ahead and loves and cares and provides, our
heavenly Father. We need not be afraid of Him! No, never afraid.

> I will both lay me down in peace, and sleep: for thou, LORD,
> only makest me dwell in safety. (Psalm 4:8)

His will is the will of love. The love of God is more tender
than the love of the best mother for her little child who nestles
in her arms and sleeps on her heart.

And then, second, this other word: Let us remember His
will is always best for us, whatever it is. God's will for us is not
only right because it is God's will, but it is best for He deals

with us from the standpoint of mercy and grace and love. His will is always best.

You may say, "There is much about it that I do not understand." Certainly. We walk by faith, not by sight. Oh, how difficult for us to walk by faith! The highest tribute to the heavenly Father is for us to walk by faith. The chiefest education that the human spirit gets in this world is in walking by faith and not by sight. Where we cannot trace God, then are we to trust Him. When we walk by faith we say, as Job said when all the lights had gone out for him, when all his defenses seemed broken down, when all hope seemed gone, "Though he slay me, yet will I trust in him" (Job 13:15).

Stonewall Jackson, great Christian soldier wounded accidentally by one of his own men, dying at the battle of Chancellorsville, said, "If I live, it will be for the best; if I die, it will be for the best. God knows and directs all things for the best for His children. God's will be done." That is exactly the way to pray.

I am thinking of a little woman long afflicted but who had marvelous faith in the eternal verities of religion. Oh, how pitiful was her physical condition. One day, realizing her serious affliction and with ever deepening sympathy, her aunt who cared for her said to her, "My dear niece, if the Lord Jesus were to ask you today to choose whether you would go on to heaven and be taken out of this world of suffering, or whether you would stay here awhile longer, you would have no trouble in making your choice, would you, dear?" She waited a moment and said, "I would ask Jesus to decide it for me, for I would not know which was the better for me." And that is exactly the thing for us to say. I would ask Him to decide it for me, whether I should get out of all this tribulation and suffering and pain and go to the House of Life and Light and Love with all the limitations of earth left behind me forever, or whether I should learn some more lessons and get some more discipline—some more of walking by faith and not by sight. We are not to be afraid to pray this prayer.

There is another truth that should be emphasized. This is a prayer, not only for those who are tested and who suffer and who are distraught and overburdened and tried in the work and experience of life, but this prayer is a call for the strong, for the heroic, for the able-bodied. This prayer is a call for cooperation with God. Your will be done. Not talked about, not submitted to, not resigned to. Your will be done. Father, Your will be translated into the life of America and throughout the world. Your will be done here on earth as it is done in heaven. It is a call for cooperation with God. A great call! We are fellow workers with Christ. Are there duties that we should perform for God? Then, we become His fellow workers if we get under the yoke with Him and go about translating into life the will of God. Are there wrong conditions about us which ought to be changed? Then, with God's help, and according to His will, it behooves us to devote our highest energies to bringing about the needed changes. In other words, if we pray, "Thy will be done," we must, to the limit of our power, seek to answer our own prayer.

Years ago, there was a dreadful scourge of typhoid fever in England and the Christian people asked the prime minister to appoint a day of prayer that this scourge might be stayed. He said, "I will gladly do so. But more than that, I will ask all the scientists to get busy and see what it is that causes this scourge of sickness which pervades old England from border to border."

Let us pray and let us also seek to rectify wrong conditions. I knew a whole family in my boyhood that went through a dreadful siege of malarial fevers. For months the awful battle went on. One would go down with it as another became well. Bye and bye the old country doctor said, "There is some local cause. Let's see what there is about this house that has caused all this trouble." And then he looked carefully and there under the house was a cellar filled with long-standing water. He said, "Let this cellar be completely cleaned out, be utterly renovated, or this sickness will persist with increasing severity." When the source of infection was removed, the scourge was ended. We are not simply to pray. We are to answer our own prayers to the limit of our powers. If we can, we are to put hands and tongue and feet and purses and loyal service with our prayers or else our prayers may be futile.

That was a great story about some neighbors who met to pray for a widow whose husband had left her with a house full of children and with very little to eat and with very little to wear. This group of big, brawny men met one Sunday afternoon to pray that conditions might be better for that poor widow and her family. Right in the middle of their prayers, a big, half-grown boy came in (the son of one of the fathers who did not come) and he put down a great sack of groceries and said, "Pa couldn't come but sent his prayers." That's what we are to do again and again. Let us fortify our prayers with service. Let us undergird our appeal with cooperation. Let us answer our prayers to the last limit of our power, and then God will do the rest.

Your will be done in earth, as it is in heaven. Your will be done in our homes. Let us begin there. And further back, let us begin with our own individual lives. Your will be done with my life, and then Your will be done in our homes, whatever that will is, without reserve. Your will be done in our church. Your will be done in our town. Your will be done in our state, in our nation, in the whole world. Whatever Your will is, oh, Father, we pray that it be brought to pass. Here are our hands, here are our feet, here are our pocketbooks, here is our loyalty, here is our love, here is our own life—all we give to You. Thus, should we pray.

We sometimes talk about the sacred and the secular. This is not proper talk for a Christian. There are no secularities in the right kind of a Christian life. "Whether therefore ye eat, or drink, or whatsoever ye do, do all to the glory of God" (1 Cor. 10:31). Go to your bank for God's glory. Go to your court house for God's glory. Go to your store for God's glory, or to the factory, or to the shop, or to the office, or to the farm. Whatever your post of service, go there for the glory of God. Whether you eat or drink, or whatsoever you do, do all for the glory of God. That is answering this prayer. That is living the life triumphant and victorious which Christ wants every one of His followers to live. Paul said, "For to me to live is Christ" (Phil. 1:21). This means, for me to live is for Christ to live in me and through me. I am His and I am to do His will for the little time He wants me to stay here in the earthly arena.

Look once more at the pattern of this prayer! "Thy will be done in earth, as it is in heaven." There is the pattern. How is God's will done in heaven? The Bible gives us a few glimpses, but they are very revealing. God's will is done joyfully in heaven. There is not a grouch in heaven, not one. Some have been grouches down here but when they entered within the gates of heaven they left all the grouches behind. Thank God for that! There will never be one pessimistic grouch heard in heaven throughout eternity. The joy of the Lord is your strength forever. "Rejoice in the Lord alway: and again I say, Rejoice" (Phil. 4:4). "In every thing by prayer and supplication with thanksgiving let your requests be made known unto God" (v. 6). And let joy brood over you and reign in you. Let us go joyfully, cheerfully, songfully about all our work. What if conditions are strenuous and exacting? What if adversity does come with its smiting duress? Behind the clouds there is One who lives and rules and reigns and loves. His will be done, and out of it all may He bring to pass that which will be best for us and for the glory of His name. And He will, if we relate ourselves thus joyfully and trustfully to Him.

How else is His will done above? It is done wholeheartedly. Surely there is no grudging service given yonder in heaven. Heaven is a busy place. Some think they will rest there, and they will. There will be no sense of weariness in that blessed home, although heaven is to be a busy place. I love to think of the activities that will be ours when we get to heaven! I think it would not be heavenly at all if there were nothing but idleness there. In fact, I think there will be no idlers there. His servants shall serve Him wholeheartedly. There will be no careless, halfhearted service on high. Often our service here in this life is limited, is grudging, is coerced. How pitiful if we give our money to Christ's cause under duress, under hesitation! How pitiful if we give our time, our talents, our cooperation to Christ and His church, grudgingly, coercedly, hesitatingly. There will be none of that in heaven.

If there will be no idlers in all that vast company of the redeemed through Christ's blood in the Father's house of many mansions, and we pray, "Thy will be done in earth, as it is in heaven," then we are praying that there be no idlers here among God's servants. What we are really praying is, "Father, help us that none of us shall be idlers. Father, help us that none of us shall be parasites here in this world. We are passing this way but once. Help us to work, to watch, and to pray. While we make this journey, Father, let us do all the good we can in all the ways we can to all the people we can down to the last hour of our journey."

And as we pray this prayer, oh, make it personal. Let us make it personal. Are you afraid to pray it? Put that fear utterly away. Morning, noon, and night pray this great prayer, "Father, Your will be done here on earth, as it is in heaven. Begin, Father, with me. Your will be done in me and through me. Whatever it means, wherever it leads, whether by life or by death, Your will be done." And then with our homes, the same way, the same prayer. And then with our city, with our state, with our nation, with all the world of suffering and needy humanity, "Your will forever be done with it all."

There are just two centers—self and Christ. Which shall it be for you? The selfish life is marked inevitably for defeat. The Christ-centered life is marked inevitably for triumph. "He always wins who sides with Christ. To Him no cause is lost." Side with Christ. Oh, hesitating soul, decide for Christ! Whatever your problem, your plight, your situation, your need, pray the great prayer and leave it unafraid in God's hand, and the right thing will come to pass as God lives.

Have thine own way, Lord,
  Have thine own way.
Thou art the potter,
  I am the clay.
Mould me and make me
  After Thy will,
While I am waiting,
  Yielded and still.

NOTES

Our Daily Bread

George H. Morrison (1866–1928) assisted the great Alexander Whyte in Edinburgh, pastored two churches, and then, in 1902, became pastor of the distinguished Wellington Church on University Avenue in Glasgow, Scotland. His preaching drew great crowds; in fact, people had to line up an hour before the services to ensure that they got seats in the large auditorium. Morrison was a master of imagination in preaching, yet his messages are solidly biblical.

From his many published volumes of sermons, I have chosen this message, found in *The Afterglow of God*, published in 1912 by Hodder and Stoughton, London.

8

Our Daily Bread

Give us this day our daily bread. (Matthew 6:11)

ONCE MORE IN THE KINDLY PROVIDENCE of God we have reached the season of the harvest. The reaper has been busy in the fields, and sower and reaper have rejoiced together. Many a day in the past summer-season we wondered if the corn would ever ripen. There was such rain, so pitiless and ceaseless. There was such absence of sunshine and of warmth. Yet, in spite of everything, harvest has arrived. The fields have been heavy with their happy burden, and in the teeth of clenched antagonisms the promises of God have been fulfilled. Every harvest is a prophecy. It is the shadow of an inward mystery. It cries to us, as with a golden trumpet, "With *God* all things are possible" (Matt. 19:26; Mark 10:27).

And so in days when all the world is dreary and excellence seems farther off than ever, the wise man will pluck up heart again as not despairing of his harvest home. Well, now I want to take our text and set it in the light of harvest. I want to look upon our daily bread against the background of the harvest field. A thing seems very different, does it not, according to the light in which you view it? Suppose then that in this light we look for a little while at these familiar words.

What the Answer to This Prayer Involves

Now when you read it unimaginatively, this seems an almost trifling petition. It almost looks like an intruder here, and men have often spoken of it so. On the one side of it is the will of God, reaching out into the height of heaven. On the other side of it are our sins, reaching down into unfathomed depths. And then, between these two infinities, spanning the distance from cherubim to Satan, is *"Give us this day our daily bread."* Our sin runs back to an uncharted past, but in this petition is no thought of yesterday. The will of God shall be forevermore, but in this petition is no tomorrow. Give us this day our daily bread—supply us with a little food today—feed us until we go to rest tonight. As if some frail and tiny cockleshell should be sailing between two mighty galleons, as if some hillock that a child could climb should be set down between two mighty Alps, so seems this prayer for our daily bread between the will of the eternal God and the cry for pardon for our sins whose roots go down into the depths of hell.

But now suppose you take this prayer and set it in the light of harvest. Give us this day our daily bread. Can you tell me what is involved when it is answered? Why, if you but realized it and caught the infinite range of its relationships, never again would it be insignificant. For all the ministry of spring is in it, and all the warmth and glory of the summer, and night and day, and heat and cold, and frost, and all the falling of the rain. And light that has come from distances unthinkable, and breezes that have blown from far away, and powers of nourishment that for a million years have been preparing in the mother earth. Give us this day our daily bread. Is it a little thing to get a piece of bread? Is it so little that it is out of place here where we are moving in the heights and depths? Not if you set it in the light of harvest, and think that not a crust can be bestowed unless the sun has shone, the rain fallen, and the earth been quietly busy for millenniums.

I think then there is a lesson here about the greatness of the things for which we pray. Our tiniest petitions might seem large if we only knew what the answer would involve. There are things that you ask for which seem little things. They are peculiar and personal and private. They are not plainly vast like some petitions, as when we pray for the conversion of the world. Yet could you follow out that prayer of yours, that little private individual prayer, you might find it calling for the power of heaven as mightily as the conversion of the nations. "Thou art coming to a king, large petitions with thee bring." Only remember that a large petition is not always measured by the compass of it. It may be small and yet it may be large. It may be trifling and be tremendous, for all the dear dead days beyond recall may somehow be implicated in the answer. You are lonely, and you pray to God that He would send a friend into your life. And then some day to you there comes that friend, perhaps in the most casual of meetings. Yet who shall tell the countless prearrangements, and the nice adjustment of a million orderings, before there was that footfall on the threshold which has made all the difference in the world to you? Give us this day our daily bread, and the sunshine and the storm are in the answer. Give us a friend, and perhaps there were no answer saving for omniscience and omnipotence. Now we know in part and see in part, but when we know even as we are known, we shall discover all that was involved in the answer to our humblest prayers.

The Toil That Lies Behind the Gift

There are some gifts that we shall always value because of the love which has suggested them. There are others that mean much to us because of the thoughtfulness which they reveal. But now and then a gift is given us that touches us in a peculiar way because we recognize the toil it cost. It may be given us by a child perhaps, or it may be given us by some poor woman. And it is not beautiful, nor is it costly, nor would it fetch a shilling in the market. And yet to us who know the story of it and how the hands were busied in the making, it may be as beautiful as any diadem. It was not purchased with an easy purse. The purses that I am thinking of are lean. It was not ordered from a foreign market. Love is not fond of trafficking in markets. In that small workshop where your boy is busy, in that small room where the poor sufferer lives, it was designed and fashioned and completed. Such gifts are often sorry to the eye. Such gifts are never sorry to the heart. Poor may they be and insignificant, yet never to us can they be insignificant. We know what they have cost, and knowing *that*, we recognize an unsuspected value. We know the toil that is behind the gift.

I want you then to take that thought and to apply it to your daily bread. It is a gift, and yet behind that gift do you remember all the toil there is? I could understand a man despising manna, even though manna was the bread of angels. It came so easily, was so lightly obtained, and was so lavishly and freely given. But daily bread is more divine than manna, for it, like manna, is the gift of heaven, and yet we get it not until arms are weary and sweat has broken on the human brow. I think of the plowman with his steaming horses driving his furrow in the heavy field. I think of the sower going forth to sow. I think of the stir and movement of the harvest. I think of the clanking of the threshing mill, of the dusty grinding of the corn, and of all those who in our baking houses are toiling in the night when we are sleeping. *Give* us this day our daily bread— then it is a gift, that daily bread. It comes to us from God in His great bounty and in His compassion for His hungry children. And yet it comes not through an opened heaven, but through the sweat and labor of humanity, through men and women who are often weary bearing the heat and burden of the day.

And is it not generally in such ways that our most precious gifts are given us? Every good and perfect gift is from above, yet is there something of heart-blood on them all. A noble painting is a precious gift. It is a thing of beauty and a joy forever. Look at it, how calm and beautiful it is. There is not a trace of struggle in its beauty. But had you lived in communion with the artist, and had you been with him when he was painting that, what strain and agony you would have seen! So is it with every noble poem, and so with our civil and religious liberty. They are all gifts to us. They come from God. They are ours to cherish and enjoy. Yet every one of them is wet with tears and characterized with human toil and pain—oftentimes, like the Messiah's garment, dipped in the final ministry of blood. Into that fellowship of lofty gifts I want you, then, to put your daily bread. It is not little, nor is it insignificant when you remember all that lies behind it. And you do not wonder now to find it here between the will of God and our transgression, though the one rises to the height of glory and the other tangles in the pit of hell.

Lastly, in the light of harvest think of the hands through which the gift is given. Give us this day our daily bread, we pray, and then through certain hands it is bestowed. Whose hands? Are they the hands of God? "No man hath seen God at any time" (John 1:18; 1 John 4:12). Are they, then, the hands of the illustrious, or of those whose names are famous in the world? All of you know as well as I do that it is not thus that our bread is ministered. It reaches us by the hands of lowly men. Out of his cottage does the reaper come, and back to his cottage does he go at evening. And we halt a moment, and we watch him toiling under the autumn sunshine in the field. But what his name is, where he had his birth, what his hopes and tragedies are, of that we know absolutely nothing. So was it with the sower in the spring. So is it with the harvester in autumn. They have no chronicle, nor any luster, nor any greatness in the eyes of man. And what I want now to realize is this, that when God answers this universal prayer, it is such hands as these that He employs. Once in Scotland we had a different story. Once we had a genius at the plow. He saw visions there and he dreamed dreams until his field was as a lawn of paradise. But for that *one*, who has his crown of amaranth, are there not tens of thousands who are nameless, toiling, sorrowing, rejoicing, dying, and never raising a ripple on the sea? Give us this day our daily bread. It is by such hands that the prayer is answered. It is by these that the Almighty Father shows that He is hearkening to His children. It is His recognition of obscurity, and of lives that are uncheered by human voices, and of days that pass in silence and in shadow into the silence and shadow of the grave.

Now have you ever quietly thought of what we owe to ministries like that? One of the deepest debts we owe is to those who are sleeping in unregarded graves. It is not the rare flower that makes the meadow beautiful. It is the flower that blossoms by the thousand there. It is not the aurora that gives the sky its glory. It is the radiance of the common day. And so with life. Perhaps we shall never know how it is beautified and raised and glorified by those who toil in undistinguished fashion. Such men may never write great poems, but it is they who make great poems possible. Such may never do heroic things, but they are the soil in which the seed is sown. Such men will not redeem the world. It takes the incarnate Son of God for that. But they—the peasants and the fishermen—will carry forth the music to humanity. Give us this day our daily bread. Are there not multitudes who are praying so? And you, you have no genius, no gifts? You are an obscure and ordinary person? But if there is any meaning in our text, set in the light of sowing and of harvest, it is that the answer to that daily prayer will be vouchsafed through lowly folk like you.

NOTES

Forgiveness

John Daniel Jones (1865–1942) served for forty years at the Richmond Hill Congregational Church in Bournemouth, England, where he ministered the Word with a remarkable consistency of quality and effectiveness, as his many volumes of published sermons attest. A leader in his denomination, he gave himself to church extension (he helped to start thirty churches), assistance to needier congregations, and increased salaries for the clergy. He spoke at D. L. Moody's Northfield Conference in 1919.

This sermon was taken from his book *The Model Prayer,* published by James Clarke and Company in 1899.

9

Forgiveness

And forgive us our debts, as we also have forgiven our debtors.
(Matthew 6:12 ASV)

And forgive us our sins; for we ourselves also forgive every one
that is indebted to us. (Luke 11:4 ASV)

MY EXPOSITION OF THE LORD'S PRAYER brings me this morning to
speak a few simple words upon the two great fundamental facts
of the gospel—man's need of forgiveness and God's willingness
to bestow it.

The petition immediately preceding this one is the prayer
for daily bread. We are absolutely dependent upon God for
our very existence, so our Lord teaches us to ask God for the
food—the material bread that is to sustain our physical life from
day to day. But "man shall not live by bread alone" (Matt. 4:4;
Luke 4:4). There is another hunger than hunger of the body—
there is a hunger of the soul. What the soul hungers for is pardon, forgiveness, and the peace that forgiveness always brings.
So when we have prayed for bread, we have not come to an
end. We have another prayer to offer. We have a larger request
to make. We have a greater boon to ask: "Give us this day our
daily bread, and forgive us our sins."

The question has often been asked, "Is life worth living?" By some the question is answered without reservation in the affirmative, by others in the negative. For myself, I am not prepared to answer either "Yes" or "No." My reply would be, "It all depends." Life, it seems to me, is not worth having if it be not lived in the sunshine of God's smile. Life is not worth having if God's face is turned away from us. Life is not worth having if our sins interpose themselves like a black frowning cloud between us and the Eternal Light. To make life worth living, life must be made happy and blessed and peaceful. Before life can be made happy, that barrier of sin must be removed, and we must walk in the light of God's countenance. The prayer for bread is a prayer for *life*—for mere *existence*. But mere existence may be a doubtful boon. To some, the prolongation of life simply means the prolongation of misery. Why should men pray for the continuance of a life which is radically wretched? There are multitudes in our world more inclined to pray for swift death than for long life. They say, with Charles Kingsley, "The sooner it's over, the sooner to sleep." No, it is not mere life, it is not life at any price, but it is the blessed, the peaceful life we want. So we go on to pray for a gift greater far than the gift of bread. We go on to pray for that which alone can make life tolerable, welcome, really worth living. We go on to pray for mercy, pardon, reconciliation, peace. "Father, forgive us our sins."

Sin is an ugly word, a word that stands for the ugliest, most terrible fact in the universe of God. The world was fair and bright until sin entered it. All its wretchedness is the result of sin. Man was pure and happy until sin entered. His foulness and brokenheartedness are the result of sin. The Bible looks at this terrible fact of sin and fails to find a single word large enough to describe it in all its many aspects of horror. It employs various words for this one terrible thing according as it views it from different standpoints. Looking at it from the standpoint of the true end of human life, sin is a "missing of the mark." The chief end of man is to glorify God. The sinner fails in that he misses the mark. Sin from this point of view means *failure, defeat, disaster*. The Bible looks at sin from the standpoint of law, the Divine Law written in the nature and on the conscience of man, and brands sin as *lawlessness*. Every single sin is a *trespass*, a transgression, an overstepping of the bounds. The Bible looks at sin from the standpoint of prudence, and stigmatizes sin as *folly*—the most stupendous and senseless of all follies. The sinner is a man who, for a few moments of delirious excitement, barters away his immortal soul. The Bible looks at sin from the standpoint of God, and sin then becomes *disobedience*, or, as in the text quoted from Matthew, it becomes *"debt."*

Perhaps we are too apt to think of sin only in its effect upon ourselves. We think of the blight it brings upon human character and the ruin it makes in human lives. It is terrible to us because it always brings a curse with it. We fear and dread sin, not always because of its own intrinsic horror, but because of the penalties it inevitably entails, so that all too often our very fear of sin has it roots in selfishness and springs out of self-love. I want to say to you that we shall never see sin in its naked horror, we shall never see it in its awful hatefulness, until we look at it from another standpoint. We sin not against ourselves alone, but *against* God. David, in the great crime of his life, had sinned against Uriah, whose blood he had caused to be shed, and against Bathsheba, the partner of his sin, and against his own soul. But when, under the faithful speech of Nathan, he was brought to see that awful sin of his in its true light, he lost sight of himself and Bathsheba and Uriah. He could think only of the God he had flouted and outraged and grieved. This was the agonized cry that broke from his lips, "Against *thee*, thee only, have I sinned, and done that which is evil in *thy* sight" (Ps. 51:4).

Then comes in the enormity of sin. It is sin *against God!* Let me illustrate what I mean from our ordinary human life. Say that a son who has been loved at home and has been the pride of his mother's heart, falls into disgrace and is brought up in the police courts charged with some shameful deed. If such a son has any sensibility at all, his sin will appear hateful to him, not so much because it has brought disgrace and loss of liberty to himself but because away at his home a mother's heart is well near broken with shame and grief. That will be the keenest stab of pain such a lad will suffer. It is the picture of his heartbroken mother that will make him loathe and despise and hate his sin. It is then we shall see the hatefulness of sin when we occupy David's standpoint and say, "Against thee, thee only have I sinned." Even though sin entailed no loss to the sinner, involved no penalty, brought with it no curse, it would remain still utterly loathsome and hateful if we only realized that every sin of ours caused grief and pain to the heart of the eternal God, our loving Father in heaven.

Now that is the point of view from which sin is regarded in this prayer. It is *against God!* Matthew uses the word *debt.* As Dr. Morrison says, "When we sin there is something in our act for which we become *liable* to God. Formerly He had a claim upon us; now He has a claim *against* us." The sins of our past history are included in this word *debt.* They have not done with us, though we try to persuade ourselves that we have done with them! Ah! what a relief it would be if we could only be sure that sin when once committed was over and done with forever! But it is not so! These sins of ours enroll themselves in a great book of accounts—not one is omitted, not one is overlooked, not one is forgotten. Do we try to persuade ourselves that somehow or other the sins of the past have been lost sight of? Do we try to flatter ourselves that they have been buried in the dust of the years? That is a vain hope. There are no mistakes, no omissions in the eternal account books. The ink of those books never fades. There every sin is enrolled. There you see them—a long, black, damning list. That is your *debt.* Sins of commission—the evil words we have spoken, the evil deeds we have done—they are all there. Sins of *omission* are there as well. In fact, I fancy that it is to sins of this class that the word *debt* specially points. *Debt* is something we *owe.* In relation to God, it is something we owed to Him and failed to pay. So it stands here for the many things we ought to have done, which we have left undone.

There are some of us who perhaps flatter ourselves that we have never committed any flagrant sin. We are not blasphemers. We are not drunkards. We are not profligates. We have never committed theft or adultery or murder. We have never been guilty of any crime that has brought us to public shame. On the strength of that we are half inclined to think that the name "sinner" is not applicable to us. But notice how this word *debt* lays hold of even the most respectable of us. There are certain things we *owe* to God. We owe Him reverence. Have we given it to Him? We owe Him obedience. Have we given it to Him? We owe Him service. Have we given it to Him? We owe Him our heart's best love. Have we given it to Him? We owe Him the first place in our thoughts and affections. Have we given it to Him? We owe Him complete self-surrender. Have we given it to Him? Ask yourselves these questions. Probe your hearts with them. Face them frankly and honestly. Have you given God perfect obedience, the best love of your hearts, the first place in your lives? Oh, how such questions humble us! How they cover us with shame and confusion!

Looking back over my own life, I can see how my years have been marred and disfigured by my failure to give to God what He has a right to expect. I can see that I have not reverenced Him as I ought. I have not obeyed Him as I ought. I have not placed Him first as I ought. When I begin to ask myself if I have done what God expects from me, my pride all disappears, my heart is pierced as with sharp swords, my self-satisfaction is torn to shreds, and I am humbled to the dust. As I look back, every day tells its tale of things left undone that I ought to have done, and these sins of omission rise up before me—a mountain load of debt that I owe to God.

Debt! What a terrible word that is to every true and honest man! There are multitudes who would prefer to bear privation and poverty rather than run into debt. The workhouse is bad enough, but better the workhouse than "debt." But will you suffer me to say that "debtors" we all of us are? "For all have sinned, and fall short of the glory of God" (Rom. 3:23). We have come short—we have given God less than His due. He has a claim against us; we are "in debt" to Him. And the debt is one that cannot be expressed in the figures and coinage of earth. It is a debt that money can never pay.

I have heard sometimes of men who, when they have found themselves in financial difficulties, have called their creditors together and have said to them, "If you will but give me time, I will pay you all in full." From time to time we read in our newspapers of honorable men discharging with interest debts they had incurred years before. Can we do something like that with this debt we owe to God? Can we work it off in the days and years that are to come? I cannot hold out to you any hope of doing that. Work as hard as you like to please God today, but when the day is done, what will you have to say? Just this, "We have been unprofitable servants. We have only done what we ought." Only what we ought—there is no margin, nothing over, that you can apply to the reduction of the old debt. The arrears of obligation are untouched. May I venture to say that, before night comes, by some sin or other you will have added to the debt? It would be as easy to bale the ocean dry as to hope by your own efforts to pay this debt. It would be as easy—no, it would be infinitely easier—to count the sands of the seashore than to remove this mountain load of obligation. Try your best, and you will fail as Paul failed, as Luther failed. In spite of your best efforts, the debt—that crushing debt—goes on increasing.

Well, what can you do? *You* can do nothing! *Sin* past and present, *sin* of commission and omission, *sin*—that long, black, damning record that stands against your name in the eternal account book—what can you do with it? How can you remove it? How can you blot it out? How can you bury it out of sight and mind? How can you erase out of the book that fatal story? You say you must have something done or that debt will strangle you. What can you do to be delivered from this body of death? My brother, you can do nothing. You cannot pay the debt. You cannot blot out the sin. You cannot erase the record from the book. Do your best and at the end you will be "in debt." But you say, " Can nothing be done? Am I then doomed to ruin and to death? Is there no way of paying this debt?" Here is the gospel in a nutshell. Here is the good news, old as the centuries, but new in your ears and mine today. Something *can* be done! *You* can do nothing. *I* can do nothing. But God, the God against whom we have sinned, He can do everything. He can remove that mountain load of debt. He can blot out that fatal record in the book. He can erase every entry. He can bury our sins out of sight forever. We can never pay that overwhelming debt. But *He,* He can give us our account back with "Settled" written at the bottom of it. Oh yes, here is the gospel: sin in man, but forgiveness in God; debt in man, but mercy in God. "Where sin abounded, grace did abound more exceedingly" (Rom. 5:20).

Listen, as to what God will do with your sins and mine! He will cancel the debt! He will blot out the handwriting that was against us and put it out of the way, nailing it to the cross of Christ! He will erase that fatal record in the book! He will remember our sins against us no more. As far as the east is from the west, so far will He remove our transgressions from us. Listen to His invitation and His gracious promise, "Come now, and let us reason together, saith Jehovah: though your sins be as scarlet, they shall be as white as snow; though they be red like crimson, they shall be as wool" (Isa. 1:18). This is the gospel—this is the good news. There is something greater, stronger even than the sin of man, and that is the grace of God. I can see a limit to human sin. I can see no limit to the Divine mercy.

> Plenteous grace with Thee is found,
> Grace to pardon all my sin.

Yes, there is mercy with God! There is forgiveness with Him! The wonder of the world still is that the God against whom we have sinned is the One who will take our sin away.

All souls that were, were forfeit once,
And He that might the vantage best have took
Found out the remedy.

That remedy was the Cross of Christ. It is He, the sinless Jesus, who has canceled the debt. "Christ died for our sins according to the scriptures" (1 Cor. 15:3). It is His pierced hand that shall blot out the record of our sins. It is in His lifeblood that we are to be washed free from every stain. It is at the foot of His cross that our sins are to be buried. Christ the sinless one is the Lamb of God. He has borne our griefs and carried our sorrows, and the Lord has laid on Him the iniquity of us all. This is the gospel. There is a debt against us we can never hope to pay. But God for Christ's sake will cancel it. There are sins that crush us with their weight and burden, but God for Christ's sake will take them all away. There are stains upon us—black and deep and foul. But the blood of Jesus Christ His Son cleanses us from all sin. Just as the snow descends from heaven and hides all the grime and filth of earth underneath its mantle until the whole surface is one pure glistening white, so God will let His mercy cover us. He will clothe us in righteousness until every stain is covered and we stand forth whiter than snow.

God was in Christ reconciling the world to Himself, not reckoning to them their trespasses. The Cross proclaims that there is forgiveness with God. And I want to preach the free, glad gospel of the Cross to you this morning. I want to say to you sin-stricken, perishing, dying men and women that there is forgiveness with God. There is nothing that His mercy cannot do. There is no sin too great, no guilt too black for Him to pardon. A poor criminal in Scotland, as he went forth to his place of execution, kept crying out, "He is a great Forgiver. He is a great Forgiver." Yes, He is a great Forgiver! Let us men and women, ruined and undone by sin, praise God, for He is a great Forgiver. His tender mercy is ever upon us. In God's mercy is our hope. And the Cross is the pledge of pardon that stoops to the lowest and most vile. The Cross, the Cross—the bitter, shameful Cross; the glorious, radiant Cross; our most jubilant songs arise from the Cross—

> E'er since by faith I saw the stream
>   His flowing wounds supply,
> Redeeming love has been my theme,
>   And shall be till I die.

Well! And what was the *price of pardon?* I can tell you what it cost God. It cost God the death of His own, His only Son. The Cross was necessary to make pardon possible. "Apart from shedding of blood there is no remission" (Heb. 9:22). That is what your forgiveness and mine cost God—it cost Him the blood of His Son. But what will it cost us? What will it cost? It will cost us *nothing*. As I said, when speaking of the previous petition, God does not sell, God *gives*. Some have tried to buy forgiveness by fasts and vigils and penances and rigid self-discipline. That is how Luther, when he was a monk at Erfurt, and Thomas Bilney, when he was a student at Cambridge, tried to obtain pardon and peace. Some have even believed that pardon was to be bought with money, so the boxes of the indulgence sellers in Germany were filled with the coins of men and women who wanted forgiveness. But pardon is not to be bought, neither with money nor penances nor vigils nor fasts. Forgiveness is to be had for nothing. Pardon is given without money and without price. All that is required is that you should *ask* for it. "Ask, and ye shall receive" (John 16:24). Zaccheus asked, and he received it. Mary of Magdala asked, and she received it. The thief on the cross asked, and he received it. Come and ask, and you, too, shall receive it. Why will you be stricken any more? Why will you die, O house of Israel. Come and ask, and you shall hear the answer fall on your ears like sweetest music: "Son, daughter, 'thy sins are forgiven. . . . Go in peace'" (Luke 7:48–50). That is what this petition teaches us to do. It bids us come and ask. For Jesus recognizes that we are all of us "debtors."

But the debt will be remitted for the asking. Therefore He teaches us to pray "Forgive us our trespasses." The ground of forgiveness is not in ourselves. It is not because of our own merit that the debt is canceled. We are saved not by works, but by grace. We are forgiven because of the boundless love that fills the heart of God, the love that found expression in the cross of Christ. Our confidence lies in the fact that God is our Father. Let us trust the Father! Let us believe the message of the Cross! Let us not hang back through doubt or fear! Let us go with boldness to the throne of grace just as we are—guilty, sin-stained, and vile. He will cast none of us out, but He will forgive us freely. His anger will be turned away and He will comfort us, and peace like a river shall flood our troubled souls!

Let me now go on to ask you to notice for a moment the qualifying clause, "As we also have forgiven our debtors," says Matthew. "For we ourselves also forgive every one that is indebted to us," says Luke. I think these words are meant to be in the first place *words of encouragement*. If man can forgive, much more can God. They remind us of that splendid verse, "If ye then, being evil, know how to give good gifts unto your children, how much more shall your Father who is in heaven give good things to them that ask him" (Matt. 7:11). We have known men who have generously and freely forgiven great wrongs committed against them. We are here told to think of the way in which even men can forgive in order that we may have faith to believe that God, who is infinitely more loving and pitiful than the best of men, can and will forgive to the uttermost.

But these words are also words of *solemn warning*. Sometimes they make the prayer die upon our lips, for they require the forgiving spirit to be in us before we ask forgiveness from God. Do you notice how this prayer, which soars to the heights, enforces also the simple everyday moralities? Look at this petition, "Forgive us our sins, *for we ourselves also forgive every one that is indebted to us.*" "For we ourselves also forgive every one." Is that true? Have you forgiven every one? Are there no grudges that you cherish? Are there no enmities in your heart? Is there no one against whom you cherish malice or ill-will? If there is ill-will against anyone in your heart, can you pray this prayer? Can you say to God, " Forgive us our sins, for we also forgive every one?" You remember how, in the striking story of the two debtors, our Lord condemned the man who could ask God to forgive him that awful debt of sin, and yet cherished an unforgiving spirit against his neighbor. Oh what a warning, a solemn warning, there is in this petition, "If ye forgive not men their trespasses, neither will your Father forgive your trespasses" (Matt. 6:15). Or look at the way Matthew puts it: "Forgive us our debts as we also forgive our debtors."

I want to ask you a plain question: "Would you really like God to forgive just in exactly the same way as you forgive your enemies?" Do you think you would? Why, is not our forgiveness all too often grudging and halfhearted? Do we not often cherish the remembrance of the offences? Do we not say, "I will forgive, but I cannot forget?" Would you like God to forgive you like that? I can never forget the words that Augustus Hare writes on this passage. He pictures an unforgiving man praying this prayer, and this is what he says:

> O God, I have sinned against Thee many times from my youth up until now. I have often been forgetful of Thy goodness. I have neglected Thy service. I have broken Thy laws. I have done many things utterly wrong against Thee. Such is my guiltiness, O Lord, in Thy sight; deal with me, I beseech Thee, even as I deal with my neighbour. He has not offended me one-tenth, one-hundredth part as much as I have offended Thee. But I cannot forgive Him. Deal with me, I beseech Thee, O Lord as I deal with him. He has been very ungrateful to me, though not a tenth, not a hundredth part as ungrateful as I have been to Thee. Yet I cannot overlook his ingratitude. Deal with me, O Lord, I beseech Thee, as I deal with him. I remember and treasure up every trifle which shows how ill he has behaved to me. Deal with me, I beseech

Thee, O Lord, as I deal with him. I am determined to take the very first opportunity of doing him an ill turn. Deal with me, I beseech Thee, O Lord, as I deal with him.

Oh, what a terrible curse such a prayer is! But may it not be that, if we cherish unkind feelings in our hearts, if we hug secret hates and enmities, when we ask God to forgive us in exactly the same way as we forgive others, we, too, may be invoking not blessing, but doom upon our own heads. Before we can pray this prayer, we need the spirit of forgiveness in our own hearts. Emerson says of Abraham Lincoln that "his heart was as big as the world, but there was no room in it for the memory of a wrong." Such must be our spirit also, the spirit that Jesus showed when on the cross He prayed, "Father, forgive them; for they know not what they do" (Luke 23:34). May God help us even now to forgive from our hearts our brothers their trespasses. Then can we draw near with boldness to the throne of grace and pray, "Father, forgive us our sins, for we ourselves also forgive every one that is indebted to us."

Lead Us Not into Temptation

Charles Haddon Spurgeon (1834–1892) is undoubtedly the most famous minister of the nineteenth century. Converted in 1850, he united with the Baptists and soon began to preach in various places. He became pastor of the Baptist church in Waterbeach, England, in 1851, and three years later he was called to the decaying Park Street Church, London. Within a short time, the work began to prosper, a new church was built and dedicated in 1861, and Spurgeon became London's most popular preacher. In 1855 he began to publish his sermons weekly; today they make up the fifty-seven volumes of *The Metropolitan Tabernacle Pulpit*. He founded a pastor's college and several orphanages.

This sermon was taken from *The Metropolitan Tabernacle Pulpit,* volume 24.

10

Lead Us Not into Temptation

Lead us not into temptation. (Matthew 6:13)

LOOKING OVER A BOOK of addresses to young people the other day, I met with the outline of a discourse that struck me as being a perfect gem. I will give it to you. The text is the Lord's prayer, and the exposition is divided into most instructive heads. "Our Father which art in heaven": *a child away from home.* "Hallowed be thy name": *a worshiper.* "Thy kingdom come": *a subject.* "Thy will be done in earth, as it is in heaven": *a servant.* "Give us this day our daily bread": *a beggar.* "And forgive us our debts as we forgive our debtors": *a sinner.* "And lead us not into temptation, but deliver us from evil": *a sinner in danger of being a greater sinner still.* The titles are in every case most appropriate and truthfully condense the petition. Now if you will remember the outline, you will notice that the prayer is like a ladder. The petitions begin at the top and go downward. "Our Father which art in heaven": a child, a child of the heavenly Father. Now to be a child of God is the highest possible position of man. "Behold, what manner of love the Father hath bestowed upon us, that we should be called the sons of God" (1 John 3:1). This is what Christ is—the Son of God, and "Our Father" is but a plural form of the very term that He uses in addressing God, for Jesus says, "Father." It is a very high, gracious, exalted position, which by faith we dare to occupy when we intelligently say, "Our Father which art in heaven." It is a step down to the next—"Hallowed be thy name." Here we have a worshiper adoring with lowly reverence the thrice holy God. A worshiper's place is a high one, but it attains not to the excellence of the child's position. Angels come as high as being worshipers, their incessant song hallows the name of God. But they cannot say, " Our Father," "for unto which of the angels said he at any time, Thou art my Son?" (Heb. 1:5). They must be content to be within one step of the highest, but they cannot reach the summit, for neither by adoption, regeneration, nor by union to Christ are they the children of God. "Abba, Father," is for men, not for angels. Therefore, the worshiping sentence of the prayer is one step lower than the opening "Our Father."

The next petition is for us as subjects, "Thy kingdom come." The subject comes lower than the worshiper, for worship is an elevated engagement wherein man exercises a priesthood and is seen in lowly but honorable estate. The child worships and then confesses the Great Father's royalty. Descending still, the next position is that of a servant, "Thy will be done in earth, as it is in heaven." That is another step lower than a subject, for her majesty the Queen has many subjects who are not her servants. They are not bound to wait upon her in the palace with personal service though they own her as their honored sovereign. Dukes and such like are her subjects, but not her servants. The servant is a grade below the subject. Everyone will own that the next petition is lower by far, for it is that of a beggar: "Give us this day our daily bread"—a beggar for bread, an everyday beggar. One who has continually to appeal to charity, even for his livelihood. This is a fit place for us to occupy who owe our all to the charity of heaven. But there is a step lower than the beggar's, and that is the sinner's place.

"Forgive" is lowlier than "give." " Forgive us our debts as we forgive our debtors." Here, too, we may each one take up his position, for no word better befits our unworthy lips than the prayer "forgive." As long as we live and sin we ought to weep and cry, "Have mercy on us, O Lord." And now, at the very bottom of the ladder, stands a sinner afraid of yet greater sin in extreme danger and in conscious weakness, sensible of past sin and fearful of it for the future. Hear him as with trembling lip he cries in the words of our text, "Lead us not into temptation, but deliver us from evil."

And yet, dear friends, though I have thus described the prayer as a going downward, downward is in matters of grace much the same as upward, as we could readily show if time permitted. At any rate, the down-going process of the prayer might equally well illustrate the advance of the divine life in the soul. The last clause of the prayer contains in it a deeper inward experience than the earlier part of it. Every believer is a child of God, a worshiper, a subject, a servant, a beggar, and a sinner. But it is not every man who perceives the allurements that beset him, or his own tendency to yield to them. It is not every child of God, even when advanced in years, who knows to the full the meaning of being led into temptation. For some follow an easy path and are seldom buffeted, and others are such tender babes that they hardly know their own corruptions. Fully to understand our text a man should have had sharp brushes in the wars and have done battle against the enemy within his soul for many a day. He who has escaped as by the skin of his teeth offers this prayer with an emphasis of meaning. The man who has felt the fowler's net about him—the man who has been seized by the adversary and almost destroyed—he prays with awful eagerness, "Lead us not into temptation."

I purpose at this time, in trying to commend this prayer to you, to notice, first of all, *the spirit that suggests such a petition;* secondly, *the trials that such a prayer deprecates;* and then, thirdly, *the lessons that it teaches.*

The Spirit That Suggests Such a Petition

What suggests such a prayer as this: "Lead us not into temptation"? First, from the position of the clause I gather, by a slight reasoning process, that it is suggested by *watchfulness.* This petition follows after the sentence, "Forgive us our debts." I will suppose the petition to have been answered, and the man's sin forgiven. What then? If you will look back upon your own lives, you will soon perceive what generally happens to a pardoned man, for "as in water face answereth to face, so the heart of man to man" (Prov. 27:19). One believing man's inner experience is like another's, and your own feelings were the same as mine. Very speedily after the penitent has received forgiveness and has the sense of it in his soul, he is tempted of the Devil, for Satan cannot bear to lose his subjects. When he sees them cross the borderline and escape out of his hand, he gathers up all his forces and exercises all of his cunning if, perchance, he may slay them at once.

To meet this special assault, the Lord makes the heart watchful. Perceiving the ferocity and subtlety of Satan's temptations, the newborn believer, rejoicing in the perfect pardon he has received, cries to God, "Lead us not into temptation." It is the fear of losing the joy of pardoned sin that thus cries out to the good Lord: "Our Father, do not suffer us to lose the salvation we have so lately obtained. Do not even subject it to jeopardy. Do not permit Satan to break our newfound peace. We have but newly escaped, do not plunge us in the deeps again. Swimming to shore, some on boards and some on broken pieces of the ship, we have come safe to land. Constrain us not to tempt the boisterous main again. Cast us not upon the rough billows any more. O God, we see the enemy advancing. He is ready if he can to sift us as wheat. Do not suffer us to be put into his sieve, but deliver us, we pray." It is a prayer of watchfulness.

Mark you, though we have spoken of watchfulness as necessary at the commencement of the Christian life, it is equally needful even to the close. There is no hour in which a believer can afford to slumber. Watch, I pray you, when you are alone for temptation, like a creeping assassin, has its dagger for solitary hearts. You must bolt and bar the door well if you would keep out the Devil. Watch yourself in public, for temptations in troops cause their arrows to fly by day. The choicest companions you can select will not be without some evil influence upon you unless you be on your guard. Remember our blessed Master's words, "What I say unto you I say unto all, Watch," and as you watch this prayer will often rise from your inmost heart:

> From dark temptations power,
> From Satan's wiles defend;
> Deliver in the evil hour,
> And guide me to the end.

It is the prayer of watchfulness.

Next, it seems to me to be the natural prayer of *holy horror at the very thought of falling again into sin.* I remember the story of a pitman who, having been a gross blasphemer, a man of licentious life and everything that was bad, when converted by divine grace was terribly afraid lest his old companions should lead him back again. He knew himself to be a man of strong passions and very apt to be led astray by others. Therefore, in his dread of being drawn into his old sins, he prayed most vehemently that sooner than ever he should go back to his old ways he might die. He did die there and then. Perhaps it was the best answer to the best prayer that the poor man could have offered. I am sure any man who has once lived an evil life, if the wondrous grace of God has snatched him from it, will agree that the pitman's prayer was not one whit too enthusiastic. It would be better for us to die at once than to live on and return to our first estate and bring dishonor upon the name of Jesus Christ our Lord. The prayer before us springs from the shrinking of the soul at the first approach of the tempter. The footfall of the fiend falls on the startled ear of the timid penitent. He quivers like an aspen leaf, and cries out, What, is he coming again? And is it possible that I may fall again? And may I once more defile these garments with that loathsome, murderous sin which slew my Lord? "O my God," the prayer seems to say, "keep me from so dire an evil. Lead me, I pray, where You will, even through death's dark valley, but do not lead me into temptation, lest I fall and dishonor You." The burned child dreads the fire. He who has once been caught in the steel trap carries the scars in his flesh and is horribly afraid of being again held by its cruel teeth.

The third feeling, also, is very apparent; namely, *diffidence of personal strength.* The man who feels himself strong enough for anything is daring, and even invites the battle which will prove his power. "Oh," says he, "I care not. They may gather about me who will. I am quite able to take care of myself and hold my own against any number." He is ready to be led into conflict, he courts the fray. Not so the man who has been taught of God and has learned his own weakness. He does not want to be tried, but seeks quiet places where he may be out of harm's way. Put him into the battle, and he will play the man. Let him be tempted, and you will see how steadfast he will be. But he does not ask for conflict as, I think, few soldiers will who know what fighting means. Surely it is only those who have never smelled gunpowder or seen the corpses heaped in bloody masses on each other that are so eager for the shot and shell, but your veteran would rather enjoy the piping times of peace. No experienced believer ever desires spiritual conflict, though perchance some raw recruits may challenge it. In the Christian, a recollection of his previous weakness—his resolutions broken, his promises unkept—makes him pray that he may not in future be severely tested. He does not dare to trust himself again. He wants no fight with Satan or with the world. But he asks that if possible he may be kept from those severe encounters, and his prayer is, "Lead us not into temptation." The wise believer shows a sacred diffidence.

No, I think I may say an utter despair of himself. Even though he knows that the power of God is strong enough for anything, yet is the sense of his weakness so heavy upon him that he begs to be spared too much trial. Hence the cry, "Lead us not into temptation."

Nor have I quite exhausted, I think, the phases of the spirit which suggests this prayer, for it seems to me to arise somewhat out of *charity*. "Charity?" say you. "How so?" Well, the connection is always to be observed, and by reading the preceding sentence in connection with it we get the words *as we forgive our debtors* and *lead us not into temptation*. We should not be too severe with those persons who have done wrong and have offended us, but pray, "Lord, lead us not into temptation." Your maidservant, poor girl, did purloin a trifle from your property. I make no excuse for her theft, but I beseech you, pause awhile before you quite ruin her character for life. Ask yourself, "Might not I have done the same had I been in her position? Lord, lead me not into temptation." It is true that it was very wrong in that young man to deal so dishonestly with your goods. Still, you know, he was under great pressure from a strong hand and yielded only from compulsion. Do not be too severe. Do not say, "I will push the matter through. I will have the law of him." No, but wait awhile. Let pity speak, let mercy's silver voice plead with you. Remember yourself, lest you also be tempted, and pray, "Lead us not into temptation."

I am afraid that as badly as some behave under temptation, others of us might have done worse if we had been there. I like, if I can, to form a kind judgment of the erring. It helps me to do so when I imagine myself to have been subject to their trials, to have looked at things from their point of view, to have been in their circumstances, and to have nothing of the grace of God to help me. Would I not have fallen as badly as they have done, or even gone beyond them in evil? May the day not come to you who show no mercy in which you may have to ask mercy for yourselves? Did I say—may it not

come to you? No, *it must* come to you. When leaving all below you will have to take a retrospective view of your life and
see much over which to mourn, to what can you appeal then
but to the mercy of God? And what if He should answer you,
"An appeal was made to *your* mercy, and you had none. As
you rendered to others so will I render to you." What answer
would you have if God were to treat you so? Would not such
an answer be just and right? Should not every man be paid in
his own coin when he stands at the judgment seat? So I think
that this prayer, "Lead us not into temptation," should often
spring up from the heart through a charitable feeling toward
others who have erred, who are of the same flesh and blood
as ourselves.

Now, whenever you see the drunkard reel through the
streets do not glory over him, but say, "Lead us not into temptation." When you take down the papers and read that men
of position have betrayed their trust for gold, condemn their
conduct if you will, but do not exult in your own steadfastness, rather cry in all humility, "Lead us not into temptation."
When the poor girl seduced from the paths of virtue comes
across your way, look not on her with the scorn that would
give her up to destruction, but say, "Lead us not into temptation." It would teach us milder and gentler ways with sinful
men and women if this prayer were as often in our hearts as
it is upon our lips.

Once more, do you not think that this prayer breathes the
spirit of *confidence*—confidence in God? "Why," says one, "I do
not see that." To me—I know not whether I shall be able to
convey my thought—to me there is a degree of very tender fa-
miliarity and sacred boldness in this expression. Of course, God
will lead me now that I am His child. Moreover, now that He
has forgiven me, I know that He will not lead me where I can
come to any harm. This my faith ought to know and believe,
and yet for several reasons there rises to my mind a fear lest
His providence should conduct me where I shall be tempted.
Is that fear right or wrong? It burdens my mind. May I go with

it to my God? May I express in prayer this misgiving of soul? May I pour out this anxiety before the great, wise, loving God? Will it not be impertinent? No, it will not, for Jesus puts the words into my mouth and says, "After this manner therefore pray ye" (Matt. 6:9).

You are afraid that He may lead you into temptation, but He will not do so. Should He see fit to try you, He will also afford you strength to hold out to the end. He will be pleased in His infinite mercy to preserve you. Where He leads it will be perfectly safe for you to follow, for His presence will make the deadliest air to become healthful. But since instinctively you have a dread lest you should be conducted where the fight will be too stern and the way too rough, tell it to your heavenly Father without reserve. You know at home if a child has any little complaint against his father it is always better for him to tell it. If he thinks that his father overlooked him the other day, or half thinks that the task his father has given him is too severe, or fancies that his father is expecting too much of him—if he does not say anything at all about it, he may sulk and lose much of the loving tenderness that a child's heart should always feel. But when the child frankly says, "Father, I do not want you to think that I do not love you or that I cannot trust you, but I have a troublous thought in my mind. I will tell it right straight out." That is the wisest course to follow and shows a filial trust. That is the way to keep up love and confidence.

So if you have a suspicion in your soul that perhaps your Father might put you into temptation too strong for you, tell it to Him. Tell it to Him, though it seems taking a great liberty. Though the fear may be the fruit of unbelief, yet make it known to your Lord, and do not harbor it sullenly. Remember that the Lord's Prayer was not made for Him, but for you; therefore, its reading matters from your standpoint and not from His. Our Lord's Prayer is not for our Lord. It is for us, His children. Children say to their fathers ever so many things that it is quite proper for them to say but that are not wise and

accurate after the measure of their parents' knowledge. Their
fathers know what their hearts mean, and yet there may be a
good deal in what they say that is foolish or mistaken. So I look
upon this prayer as exhibiting that blessed childlike confidence
that tells out to its father a fear that grieves it, regardless of
whether that fear be altogether correct. Beloved, we need not
here debate the question whether God leads into temptation,
or whether we can fall from grace. It is enough that we have a
fear and are permitted to tell it to our Father in heaven. Whenever you have a fear of any kind, hurry off with it to Him who
loves His little ones, and, like a father, pities them and soothes
even their needless alarms.

Thus, I have shown that the spirit that suggests this prayer
is that of watchfulness, of holy horror at the very thought of
sin, of diffidence of our own strength, of charity toward others, and of confidence in God.

The Trials That Such a Prayer Deprecates

Secondly, let us ask, what are these temptations which the
prayer deprecates? Or say rather, what are these trials which
are so much feared?

I do not think the prayer is intended at all to ask God to
spare us from being afflicted for our good, or to save us from
being made to suffer as a chastisement. Of course, we should
be glad to escape those things. But the prayer aims at another
form of trial and may be paraphrased thus: "Save me, O Lord,
from such trials and sufferings as may lead me into sin. Spare
me from too great trials, lest I fall by their overcoming my
patience, my faith, or my steadfastness."

Now, as briefly as I can, I will show you how men may be
led into temptation by the hand of God.

And the first is *by the withdrawal of divine grace.* Suppose
for a moment—it is only a supposition—suppose that the Lord
were to leave us altogether, then would we perish speedily.
But suppose—and this is not a barren supposition—that He
were in some measure to take away His strength from us,

would we not be in an evil case? Suppose that He did not support our faith, what unbelief we would exhibit? Suppose that He refused to support us in the time of trial so that we no longer maintained our integrity. What would become of us? Ah, the most upright man would not be upright long, nor the most holy, holy any more. Suppose, dear friend—you who walk in the light of God's countenance and bear life's yoke so easily because He sustains you—suppose that His presence were withdrawn from you. What must be your portion? We are all so like to Samson in this matter that I must bring him in as the illustration, though he has often been used for that purpose by others. So long as the locks of our head are unshorn, we can do anything and everything. We can rend lions, carry gates of Gaza, and smite the armies of the alien. It is by the divine consecrating mark that we are strong in the power of His might. But if the Lord be once withdrawn and we attempt the work alone, then are we as weak as the tiniest insect. When the Lord has departed from you, O Samson, what are you more than another man? Then the cry, "the Philistines be upon thee, Samson" (Judg. 16:9, 12, 14, 20) is the knell of all your glory. You do vainly shake those lusty limbs of yours. Now you will have your eyes put out and the Philistines will make sport of you. In view of a like catastrophe, we may well be in an agony of supplication. Pray then, "Lord, leave me not, and lead me not into temptation by taking Your Spirit from me."

> Keep us, Lord, oh keep us ever,
> Vain our hope if left by thee
> We are thine, oh leave us never,
> Till thy face in heaven we see;
> There to praise thee
> Through a bright eternity.

> All our strength at once would fail us,
> If deserted, Lord, by thee;

> Nothing then could aught avail us,
>   Certain our defeat would be:
>   Those who hate us
>   Thenceforth their desire would see.

Another set of temptations will be found in *providential conditions*. The words of Agur, the son of Jakeh, shall be my illustration here. "Remove far from me vanity and lies; give me neither poverty nor riches; feed me with food convenient for me lest I be full, and deny thee, and say, Who is the Lord? or lest I be poor, and steal, and take the name of my God in vain." Some of us have never known what actual want means, but have from our youth up lived in social comfort. Ah, dear friends, when we see what extreme poverty has made some men do, how do we know that we would not have behaved even worse if we had been as sorely pressed as they? We may well shudder and say, "Lord, when I see poor families crowded together in one little room where there is scarcely space to observe common decency, when I see hardly bread enough to keep the children from crying for hunger, when I see the man's garments wearing out upon his back and by far too thin to keep out the cold, I pray thee subject me not to such trial lest if I were in such a case I might put forth my hand and steal. Lead me not into the temptation of pining want."

And, on the other hand, look at the temptations of money when men have more to spend than they can possibly need, and there is around them a society which tempts them into racing and gambling and whoredom and all manner of iniquities. The young man who has a fortune ready to hand before he reaches years of discretion, and is surrounded by flatterers and tempters all eager to plunder him, do you wonder that he is led into vice and becomes a ruined man morally? Like a rich galleon waylaid by pirates, he is never out of danger. Is it a marvel that he never reaches the port of safety? Women tempt him, men flatter him, vile messengers of the Devil fawn upon him, and the young simpleton goes after them like an ox to the slaughter or as a bird hastens to the snare and knows not that it is for his life. You may very well thank heaven that you never knew the temptation, for if it were put in your way you would also be in sore peril. If riches and honor allure you, follow not eagerly after them, but pray, "Lead us not into temptation."

Providential positions often try men. There is a man very much pushed for ready money in business. How shall he meet that heavy bill? If he does not meet it, there will be desolation in his family. The mercantile concern from which he now draws his living will be broken up. Everybody will be ashamed of him. His children will be outcasts, and he will be ruined. He has only to use a sum of trust money. He has no right to risk a penny of it, for it is not his, but still by its temporary use he may perchance tide over the difficulty. The Devil tells him he can put it back in a week. If he does touch that money it will be a roguish action. But then he says, "Nobody will be hurt by it, and it will be a wonderful accommodation," and so on. If he yields to the suggestion and the thing goes right, there are some who would say, "Well, after all, there was not much harm in it. It was a prudent step, for it saved him from ruin." But if it goes wrong and he is found out, then everybody says, "It was a shameful robbery. The man ought to be transported." But the action was wrong in itself, and the consequences neither make it better nor worse. Do not bitterly condemn, but pray again and again, "Lead us not into temptation. Lead us not into temptation."

You see, God does put men into such positions in providence at times that they are severely tried. It is for their good that they are tried, and when they can stand the trial, they magnify His grace, and they themselves become stronger men. The test has beneficial uses when it can be borne, and God therefore does not always screen His children from it. Our heavenly Father has never meant to cuddle us up and keep us out of temptation, for that is no part of the system that He has wisely arranged for our education. He does not mean us to be babies in go-carts all our lives. He made Adam and Eve in the garden. He did not put an iron palisade around the Tree of Knowledge of Good and Evil and say, "You cannot get at it." No, He warned them not to touch the fruit, but they could reach the tree if they would. He meant that they should have the possibility of attaining the dignity of voluntary fidelity if they remained steadfast, but they lost it by their sin. God means in His new creation not to shield His people from every kind of test and trial, for that would breed hypocrites and keep even the faithful weak and dwarfish. The Lord does sometimes put the chosen where they are tried, and we do right to pray, "Lead us not into temptation."

And there are temptations arising out of *physical conditions.* There are some men who are very moral in character because they are in health. There are other men who are very bad, who, I do not doubt, if we knew all about them, would have some little leniency shown them because of the unhappy conformation of their constitution. Why, there are many people to whom to be cheerful and to be generous is no effort whatsoever, while there are others who need to labor hard to keep themselves from despair and misanthropy. Diseased livers, palpitating hearts, and injured brains are hard things against which to struggle. Does that poor old lady complain? She has had the rheumatism only thirty years, and yet she now and then murmurs! How would you be if you felt her pains for thirty minutes? I have heard of a man who complained of everybody. When he came to die, and the doctors opened his skull they found a close-fitting brain-box and that the man suffered from an irritable brain. Did not that account for a great many of his hard speeches? I do not mention these matters to excuse sin but to make you and myself treat such people as gently as we can. We should pray, "Lord, do not give me such a brain-box, and do not let me have such rheumatisms or such pains, because upon such a rack I may be much worse than they are. Lead us not into temptation."

So, again, *mental conditions* often furnish great temptations.

When a man becomes depressed, he becomes tempted. Those among us who rejoice much often sink about as much as we rise, and when everything looks dark around us, Satan is sure to seize the occasion to suggest despondency. God forbid that we should excuse ourselves, but, dear friend, pray that you be not led into this temptation. Perhaps if you were as much a subject of nervousness and sinking of spirit as the friend you blame for his melancholy, you might be more blameworthy than he, therefore pity rather than condemn.

And, on the other hand, when the spirits are exhilarated and the heart is ready to dance for joy, it is very easy for levity to step in and for words to be spoken amiss. Pray the Lord not to let you rise so high nor sink so low as to be led into evil. "Lead us not into temptation" must be our hourly prayer.

Further than this, there are temptations arising out of *personal associations,* which are formed for us in the order of providence. We are bound to shun evil company, but there are cases in which, without fault on their part, persons are made to associate with bad characters. I may instance the pious child whose father is a swearer and the godly woman, lately converted, whose husband remains a swearer and blasphemes the name of Christ. It is the same with workmen who have to labor in workshops where lewd fellows at every half-a-dozen words let fall an oath and pour forth that filthy language that shocks us every day more and more. I think that in London our working people talk more filthily than ever they did. At least, I hear more of it as I pass along or pause in the street. Well, if persons are obliged to work in such shops or to live in such families, there may come times when under the lash of jest and sneer and sarcasm the heart may be a little dismayed and the tongue may refuse to speak for Christ. Such a silence and cowardice are not to be excused, yet do not censure your brother, but say, "Lord, lead me not into temptation." How do you know that you would be more bold?

Peter quailed before a talkative maid, and you may be cowed by a woman's tongue. The worst temptation for a young

Christian that I know of is to live with a hypocrite—a man so sanctified and demure that the young heart, deceived by appearances, fully trusts him while the wretch is false at heart and rotten in life. And such wretches there are who, with the pretense and affectation of sanctimoniousness, will do deeds at which we might weep tears of blood. Young people are frightfully staggered, and many of them become deformed for life in their spiritual characteristics, through associating with such beings as these. When you see faults caused by such common but horrible causes, say to yourself, "Lord, lead me not into temptation. I thank You for godly parents and for Christian associations and for godly examples. But what might I have been if I had been subjected to the very reverse? If evil influences had touched me when like a vessel I was upon the wheel, I might have exhibited even grosser failings than those which I now see in others."

Thus, I might continue to urge you to pray, dear friends, against various temptations. But let me say, the Lord has for some men very *special tests,* such as may be seen in the case of Abraham. He gives him a son in his old age, and then says to him, "Take now thy son, thine only son Isaac, whom thou lovest . . . and offer him there for a burnt offering" (Gen. 22:2). You will do right to pray, "Lord, lead me not into such a temptation as that. I am not worthy to be so tried. Oh do not so test me." I have known some Christians to sit down and calculate whether they could have acted as the patriarch did. It is very foolish. When you are called upon to do it, you will be enabled to make the same sacrifice by the grace of God. But if you are not called upon to do it, why should the power be given? Shall God's grace be left unused? Your strength shall be equal to your day, but it shall not exceed it. I would have you ask to be spared the sterner tests.

Another instance is to be seen in Job. God gave Job over to Satan with a limit, and you know how Satan tormented him and tried to overwhelm him. If any man were to pray, "Lord, try me like Job," it would be a very unwise prayer. "Oh, but I could be as patient as he," you say. You are the very man who would yield to bitterness and curse your God. The man who could best exhibit the patience of Job would be the first, according to his Lord's bidding, to fervently pray, "Lead us not into temptation." Dear friends, we are to be prepared for trial if God wills it, but we are not to court it. But we are rather to pray against it, even as our Lord Jesus, though ready to drink the bitter cup, yet in an agony exclaimed, "If it be possible, let this cup pass from me." Trials sought after are not such as the Lord has promised to bless. No true child asks for the rod.

To put my meaning in a way in which it will be clearly seen, let me tell an old story. I have read in history that two men were condemned to die as martyrs in the burning days of Queen Mary. One of them boasted very loudly to his companion of his confidence that he would play the man at the stake. He did not mind the suffering. He was so grounded in the gospel that he knew he would never deny it. He said that he longed for the fatal morning even as a bride for the wedding. His companion in prison in the same chamber was a poor trembling soul who could not and would not deny his Master, but he told his companion that he was very much afraid of the fire. He said he had always been very sensitive of suffering, and he was in great dread that when he began to burn the pain might cause him to deny the truth. He besought his friend to pray for him, and he spent his time very much in weeping over his weakness and crying to God for strength. The other continually rebuked him and chided him for being so unbelieving and weak. When they both came to the stake, he who had been so bold recanted at the sight of the fire and went back ignominiously to an apostate's life, while the poor trembling man whose prayer had been, "Lead me not into temptation," stood firm as a rock, praising and magnifying God as he was burned to a cinder. Weakness is our strength, and our strength is weakness. Cry unto God that He try you not beyond your strength, and in the shrinking tenderness of your conscious weakness breathe out the prayer, "Lead us not into temptation." Then, if He does lead you into the conflict, His Holy Spirit will strengthen you, and you will be brave as a lion before the adversary. Though trembling and shrinking within yourself before the throne of God, you would confront the very Devil and all the hosts of hell without one touch of fear. It may seem strange, but so the case is.

The Lessons That This Prayer Teaches

And now I conclude with the last head: the lessons that this prayer teaches. I have not time to enlarge. I will just throw them out in the rough.

The first lesson from the prayer, "Lead us not into temptation," is this: *Never boast your own strength.* Never say, "Oh, I shall never fall into such follies and sins. They may try me, but they will find more than a match in me." Let not him that puts on his harness boast as though he were putting it off. Never indulge one thought of congratulation as to self-strength. You have no power of your own, you are as weak as water. The Devil has only to touch you in the right place and you will run according to his will. Only let a loose stone or two be moved and you will soon see that the feeble building of your own natural virtue will come down at a run. Never court temptation by boasting your own capacity.

The next thing is, *never desire trial.* Does anybody ever do that? Yes, I heard one say the other day that God had so prospered him for years that he was afraid he was not a child of God. He found that God's children were chastised, and, therefore, he almost wished to be afflicted. Dear brother, do not wish for that. You will meet with enough trouble soon enough. If I were a little boy at home, I do not think I would say to my brother because he had been whipped, "I am afraid I am not my father's child, and fear that he does not love me because I am not smarting under the rod. I wish he would whip me just to let me know his love." No. No child would ever be so stupid. We must not for any reason desire to be afflicted or tried, but must pray, "Lead us not into temptation."

The next thought is, *never go into temptation.* The man who prays, "Lead us not into temptation," and then goes into it is a liar before God. What a hypocrite a man must be who utters this prayer and then goes off to the theater! How false is he who offers this prayer and then stands at the bar and drinks and talks with depraved men and bedizened girls! "Lead us not into temptation" is shameful profanity when it comes from the lips of men who resort to places of amusement whose moral tone is bad. "Oh," you say, "you should not tell us of such things." Why not? Some of you do them, and I make bold to rebuke evil wherever it is found, and shall do so while this tongue can move. People go to church and say, "Lead us not into temptation." Then they know where temptation is to be found, and they go straight into it. *You* need not ask the Lord not to lead you there; He has nothing to do with it. The Devil and you will go far enough without mocking God with your hypocritical prayers. The man who goes into sin willfully with his eyes open, and then bends his knee and says half-a-dozen times over in his church on a Sunday morning, "Lead us not into temptation," is a hypocrite without a mask upon him. Let him take that home to himself, and believe that I mean to be personal to him and to such barefaced hypocrites as he.

The last word is, if you pray for God not to lead you into temptation, *do not lead others there.* Some seem to be singularly forgetful of the effect of their example, for they will do evil things in the presence of their children and those who look up to them. Now, I pray, consider that by ill example you destroy others as well as yourself. Do nothing, my dear brother, of which you have need to be ashamed or which you would not wish others to copy. Do the right at all times, and do not let Satan make a "cat's paw" of you to destroy the souls of others. Do you pray, "Lead us not into temptation"? Then do not lead your children there. They are invited during the festive season to such and such a family party where there will be everything but what will conduce to their spiritual growth or even to their good morals. Do not allow them to go. Put your foot down.

Be steadfast about it. Having once prayed, "Lead us not into temptation," act not the hypocrite by allowing your children to go into it.

God bless these words to us. May they sink into our souls. If any feel that they have sinned, oh that they may now ask forgiveness through the precious blood of Christ and find it by faith in Him. When they have obtained mercy, let their next desire be that they may be kept in the future from sinning as they did before, and therefore let them pray, "Lead us not into temptation." God bless you.

NOTES

Thine Is the Kingdom

Alexander Maclaren (1826–1910) was one of Great Britain's most famous preachers. While pastoring the Union Chapel, Manchester (1858–1903), he became known as "the prince of expository preachers." Rarely active in denominational or civic affairs, Maclaren invested his time in studying the Word in the original languages and in sharing its truths with others in sermons that are still models of effective expository preaching. He published a number of books of sermons and climaxed his ministry by publishing his monumental *Expositions of Holy Scripture*.

This message was taken from volume 6 of *Expositions of Holy Scripture*, published by Funk and Wagnalls in 1902 and reprinted by Baker Book House in 1974.

11

Thine Is the Kingdom

Thine is the kingdom, and the power, and the glory, for ever. Amen. (Matthew 6:13)

THERE IS NO REASON to suppose that this doxology was spoken by Christ. It does not occur in any of the oldest and most authoritative manuscripts of Matthew's gospel. It does not seem to have been known to the earliest Christian writers. Long association has for us intertwined the words inextricably with our Lord's Prayer, and it is a wound to reverential feeling to strike out what so many generations have used in their common supplications. No doubt this doxology is appropriate as a conclusion and serves to give an aspect of completeness. It sounds cold and cheerless to end our prayer with "evil." But the question is not one of feeling or of our notions of fitness, but purely one of criticism. The only evidence that has any right to be heard in settling the text of the New Testament is dead against this clause. If we regard that evidence, we are obliged to say that the doxology has no business here. How it stands here is a question that may be answered satisfactorily. When the Lord's Prayer came to be used in public worship, it was natural to append to it a doxology, just as in chanting the psalms it became the habit to repeat at the end of each the Gloria.

This doxology, originally written on the margin of the gospel, would gradually creep into the text, and once there, was naturally retained.

It does not follow that, because Christ did not speak it, we ought not to use it. It should not be in the Bible, but it may well be in our prayers. If we think that our Lord gave us a pattern rather than a form, we are quite justified in extending that pattern by any additions that harmonize with its spirit. If we think He gave us a form to be repeated *verbatim,* then we ought not to add to it this doxology.

At first sight, it seems as if the prayer without it were incomplete. It contains loving desires, lowly dependence, humble penitence, earnest wishes for cleansing, but there appears none of that rapturous praise that is also an element in all true devotion. And this may have been one reason for the addition of the doxology. But I think that that absence of praise and joy is only apparent. The first clause of the prayer expresses the highest form of both. The doxology, if you will think of it, adds nothing to the contemplation of the divine character that the prayer has already taught us. It is only a repetition at the close of what we had at the beginning, and its conception, lofty and grand as it is, falls beneath that of "Our Father." We might almost say that the doxology is incongruous with the prayer as presenting a less blessed, spiritual, distinctively Christian thought of God. That would be going too far. But I cannot but feel a certain change in tone, a dropping from the loftiest elevation down to the celebration of the lower aspects of the divine. "Kingdom, power, and glory" are grand, but they do not reach the height of ascription of praise that sounds in the very first words of the prayer.

Properly speaking, too, this doxology is not a part of the prayer. It expresses two things: the devout contemplation of God that the whole course of the petitions has excited in the soul—and in that aspect it is the church's echo to the Lord's Prayer; and the confidence with which we pray—and in that aspect it is rather the utterance of meditative reflection asking of itself its reasons for hope and stirring itself up to lay hold on God.

The Meaning of the Doxology

Kingdom, *power*, and *glory* in the last part correspond to *kingdom*, *will*, and *hallowing* in the first part. The order is not the same, but it is still substantially identical.

"Thine the kingdom." All earthly things, the whole fates of men here, are ruled by Him. The prayer asked that it might be so; here we declare that it is so already, not, of course, in the deepest sense, but that even now and here He rules with authority. "Thy kingdom is an everlasting kingdom" (Ps. 145:13), and this conviction is inseparable from our Christianity. How hard it is to believe it at all times from what we see around us! The temptation is to think that the kingdom is men's or belongs to blind fate or chance, and our own evil hearts ever suggest that the kingdom is our own. Satan said, "All is mine, and I will give it Thee."

The affairs of the world seem so far from God. We are so tempted to believe that He is remote from it, that nations and their rulers and the field of politics are void of Him. We see craft and force and villainy ruling. We see kingdoms far from any perception that society is for man and from God. We see *Dei gratiâ* on our coins but "by the grace of the Devil" for real motto. We see long tracks of godless crime and mean intrigue, and here and there a divine gleam falling from some heroic deed of sacrifice. We see king and priest playing into each other's hands, and the people destroyed, whatever be the feud. But we are to believe that the world is the kingdom of God; to learn whence comes all human rule, and to be sure that even here and now "Thy kingdom is an everlasting kingdom."

"Thine the power." Not merely has He authority over, but He works indeed through all—the whole world and all creatures are the field of the ever-present energy of God. That is a simple truth, deep but clear, that all power comes from Him. He is the cause of all changes, physical and all other. Force is the garment of the present God and among men all power is from Him. His will is the creative word.

"Thine the glory." God's glory is the praise that comes from the accomplishment of His purpose and will. This is the end of all Creation and manifestation. The thought of Scripture is that all things are for the greater glory of God. It may be a most cold-blooded and cruel doctrine, or it may be a most blessed one. All depends on what is our conception of the character of the God whose self-revelation is His glory.

An almighty Devil is the god of many people. But we have learned to say "Our Father," and hence this thought is blessed. Unless we had so learned, the thought that His end was His glory would make Him a selfish tyrant. But since we know Him to be our Father, we know that His Glory is the revelation of His Love, His Fatherhood. When we say that He does all things for His own glory, we say that He does all things that men may know His character as it is, and "to know Him is life eternal."

"Thine is the kingdom, and the power, and the glory." Whatsoever we may have lost and suffered in the past, whatsoever fiery baptism and strife of arms or of principles we may yet have to go through, whatsoever shocks of loss and sorrow may strike upon our own hearts, whatsoever untraversed seas our nation or our race may have to embark upon, One abides, the same One remains ours and is ever with us. We may have to face storm and cloud, and "neither sun nor stars may appear." We may have to fling out the best anchors we can find, if haply they may hold on anything, and may wearily "wish for the day." But "the LORD sitteth upon the flood" (Ps. 29:10). And in the thickest of the night, when we lift our wearied eyes, we shall see Him coming to us across the storm. We shall see the surges smoothing themselves to rest for His pavement and the waves subside into their caves at His voice.

"Thine is the kingdom, and the power, and the glory." Then the world and we shall be guided right and kept safe. Whatsoever is true and good shall rule. The weak cause shall be the conquering, all false fame shall fade like morning mist, and every honest desire and effort for man's blessedness shall have eternal honor. God is King; God is mighty; God's name shall have glory. Then for us there is Hope invincible in spite of all evil. Courage to stand by His truth and His will, endless patience and endless charity are our fitting robes, the livery of our King. Because He is our Father, He will deliver us from all evil. By His all-powerful love He will found His universal kingdom and get the glory due to His name, the glory of loving and being loved by all His children.

The Force of the Doxology in Its Place Here

It reminds us that the ground of our confidence is in God's own character. We do not need to make ourselves worthy to receive. We cannot move Him, but He is self-moved, and so we do not need to be afraid. Nor is our prayer to be an attempt to bend His will.

Our confidence digs deep down to build on the rock of the ever-living God, whose "is the kingdom, and the power, and the glory, for ever." We flee to Him for a refuge against ourselves. We bring nothing. We look to His own character, which will always be the same, and to His past, which is the type and prophecy for all His future. He is His own reason, His own motive, His own end.

When we ground our prayers on Him, then we touch ground. In whatever weltering sea of trouble we may be buffeted, we have found the bottom and can stand firm.

But the *Amen* that closes the doxology is not the empty form that it has now become. It means not only "So may it be!" but also "So will it be!" It is not only the last breathing of desire but also the expression of assured expectancy and confidence—not merely be it so, but confident expression of assurance that it will be so.

How much of our prayer flies off into empty air because there is no expectation in it! How much has no certainty of being answered in it! How much is followed by no marking of the future to discern the answer! We should stand praying like some Grecian statue of an archer, with hand extended and lips parted and eye following the arrow of our prayer on its flight until it touches the mark. We have a right to be confident that we shall be heard. We should apply the *Amen* to all of the petitions of the prayer. So it becomes a prophecy, and the Christian man is to live in the calm expectation that all of the petitions will be accomplished. For the world they will be, for us they may be. It is for each of us to decide for ourselves whether they will be answered in and for us.

The place of the doxology here suggests that all prayer should lead to thankful contemplation of God's character.

We have seen how the prayer begins with contemplation and then passes into supplication. Thus, all prayer should end as it began. It has a circular motion. Starting from the highest heavens and coming down to earth is thither drawn again and rests at the throne of God, where it set out, like the strong spirits before His throne who veil their faces while they gaze upon the glory and then fly forth to help human sorrows and satisfy human hearts. Then on unwearied pinions winging their way to their first station, meekly sink their wings of flight and veil their faces again with their wings. The rivers that flow through broad lands, bringing blessing and doing humble service in drinking-cup and domestic vessel, came in soft rain from heaven. Though their bright waves are browned with soil and made opaque with many a stain, yet, their work done, they rest in the great ocean and thence are drawn up once more to the clouds of heaven. So with our prayers. They ought to start from the contemplation of our God, and they ought to return there again.

And as this is the last word of our prayers, so may we not say that it represents the perpetual form of fellowship with God? Prayers for bread and pardon, and help and deliverance are for the wilderness. Prayers for the hallowing of His name, the coming of His kingdom, and the doing of His will are out of date when they are fulfilled. But forever this vo.. shall rise before His throne, and that last new song, which shall ring with might as of thunder and sweetness as of many harps from the thousand times ten thousand, shall be but the expansion and the deepening of the praise of earth. Then "every creature which is in heaven, and on the earth, and under the earth, and such as are in the sea, and all that are in them, heard I saying, Blessing, and honour, and glory, and power, be unto him that sitteth upon the throne, and unto the Lamb for ever and ever" (Rev. 5:13).

So we finish these meditations. I have felt all along how poorly my words served me to say even what I saw, and how poorly my vision saw into the clear depths of the divine prayer. But I hope that they may have helped you half as much as they have myself to feel more strongly how all-comprehensive it is. I said at the beginning, and I repeat with more emphasis now, that there is everything in this prayer: God's relations to man, man's to God and his fellows; the foundation stones of Christian theology, morals, society, and politics. There is help for the smallest wants and light for daily duties. There is strength for the hour of death and the Day of Judgment. There is the revelation of the timeless depths of our Father's heart. There is the prophecy of the furthest future for ourselves and our brothers and sisters. No man can exhaust it. Every age may find in its simple syllables lessons for their new perplexities and duties. It will not be outgrown in heaven. But, thank God, we do not need to exhaust its meaning to use it aright. Jesus interprets our prayers, and many a dumb yearning, and many a broken sob, and many a passionate fragment of a cry, and many an ignorant desire that may appear to us very unlike His pattern for all ages will be accepted by Him. He inspires, presents, and answers every prayer offered through Him to the Father in heaven. He counts the poorest prayer to be "after this manner," if it comes from a heart seeking the Father, owning its sin, longing dimly for deliverance and purity, and hoping through its tears in the great and loving tenderness of the Father in heaven who has sent His Son, that through Him we might cry Abba, Father.

The Two Worlds

George H. Morrison (1866–1928) assisted the great Alexander Whyte in Edinburgh, pastored two churches, and then in 1902 became pastor of the distinguished Wellington Church on University Avenue in Glasgow, Scotland. His preaching drew great crowds; in fact, people had to line up an hour before the services to ensure that they got seats in the large auditorium. Morrison was a master of imagination in preaching, yet his messages are solidly biblical.

From his many published volumes of sermons, I have chosen this message, found in *The Gateway of the Stars,* published in 1927 by Hodder and Stoughton, London.

12

The Two Worlds

Give us this day our daily bread. And forgive us our debts.
(Matthew 6:11–12)

WHEN OUR LORD BIDS US PRAY for daily bread, He accepts the visible world of space and time. He reveals to us our right relationship to the material world with which we are surrounded. Only if a man accepts that world is it possible for him to live. He must receive and assimilate the nourishment it offers him if his bodily life is to continue. He does not create his own material nourishment. He finds it in the world around him, and, finding it, draws it within himself. Our true attitude to that outward world lies in receiving what it has to offer us. We need bread, and it comes to us with bread. We need water, and it brings us water. Not out of the stores of our own being, but out of the vast largesse of the world, do we secure our bodily existence. All this is implied when we are taught to pray, "Give us this day our daily bread." Our Lord is not setting the bounty of His Father over against the world in which we live. He is teaching us what He profoundly felt, that the material things which make our being possible are the free gifts of a loving Father's hand.

But to our Lord there was another world, and that other world is not far away. The moment He teaches us to ask forgiveness

He has stepped from the one into the other. In the material world pardon is unknown, just because sin is nonexistent there. The effects of sin darken and disorder it, but it is not the sin of any bird or beast. These, guided by instinct, ignorant of evil, untouched by the glory of responsibility, have never felt the shamefulness of sin. The moment our Savior speaks about forgiveness He has passed into another world. It is not the world that bears the golden corn, nor is its music the music of the river. And the wonderful thing is how our blessed Lord, in a single breath, if I might put it so, moves over from the one world to the other. When He bids us pray, "Give us this day our daily bread," He is thinking of the sower and the reaper. When He bids us pray for pardon, He has moved into the realm of spirit. And quite evidently, from His swift transition, the latter was not a world of distant frontiers. It was closer than breathing, nearer than hands and feet.

Now it seems to me that this rich collocation has a profound significance for all of us. It means that to these two different worlds our attitude is meant to be identical. We crave for bread, and the one world gives us bread. We thirst for water, and it gives us water. If we are to maintain our bodily existence we must receive what we cannot create. And in the same way our deeper life, to which we give the name of spiritual, must be sustained by constant receptivity. We do not win bread out of our inward stores. We get it from the bounty of the world. It is scattered across a thousand fields, and from these fields we wrest it and assimilate it. And all the nurture of our deeper life, to which our Savior gives the name of bread, has to be received in the same way. It is not within our power to create pardon any more than it is in our power to create corn. Both are gifts and miracles of mercy, to be humbly accepted from God's hand. Give us our daily bread and forgive us. God's gifts are diverse; man's attitude is one.

One feels, too, that in this collocation is a powerful encouragement to faith. It reminds us of our Savior's graciousness in comparing faith to a grain of mustard seed. I crave for bread, and the one world comes to me crying, "Child, I have bread for you. I have satisfaction for that hunger in the loving foreordering of God." And I cannot believe that in the world of sense God would make ample provision for our cravings and mock them in the other world of spirit. You do not exhaust the hungering of man when you satisfy the hunger of his body. The craving for truth and love and light is as real as the craving for the loaf. And that God in His merciful provision should give the loaf and deny the spiritual bread to the thoughtful mind is utterly incredible. To do that would be to mock us. It would force us back to the level of the beast. To give the lower and refuse the higher would be the death-knell of the hopes of man. And how unthinkable that would have been to Jesus is evident from the one simple fact that His hopes for man are boundless. To Him, the bounty of the world of sense was a pledge of the bounty of the other world. If from the one realm we get the gift of bread, shall we not from the other get the gift of pardon? Every field ripening to the harvest and every fountain with its bubbling waters was to Him a sacrament of the world unseen where are the water and the bread of life.